CHANGES TO UNITED STATES NAVY SUBMARINE DESIGN AND CONSTRUCTION DURING WORLD WAR I, AS DETERMINED BY THE GENERAL BOARD

DAVID R. YOCUM, LCDR, U.S. NAVY

NIMBLE BOOKS LLC: THE AI LAB FOR BOOK-LOVERS
~ FRED ZIMMERMAN, EDITOR ~
Humans and AI making books richer, more diverse, and more surprising.

Publishing Information

(c) 2023 Nimble Books LLC
ISBN: 978-1-60888-277-9

AI-generated Keyword Phrases

United States Navy submarine design; World War I; Board discussions; submarine size; propulsion systems; armament considerations; habitability systems; submarine technology improvements; listening devices use; gyrocompasses implementation; hydrophones development; radio sets integration; General Board of the US Navy influence on submarine design and development; Germany's unrestricted submarine warfare response by the US Navy; more capable submarines development.

Publisher's Notes

This annotated edition illustrates the capabilities of the AI Lab for Book-Lovers to add context and ease-of-use to manuscripts. It includes five types of abstracts, building from simplest to more complex: TLDR (one word), ELI5, TLDR (vanilla), Scientific Style, and Action Items; three essays to increase viewpoint diversity: Grounds for Dissent, Red Team Critique, and MAGA Perspective; and Notable Passages and Nutshell Summaries for each page.

ANNOTATIONS

Publishing Information ii
AI-generated Keyword Phrases ii
Publisher's Notes ii
Abstracts iv
    TL;DR (one word) iv
    Explain It To Me Like I'm Five Years Old iv
    TL;DR (vanilla) iv
    Scientific Style iv
    Action Items v
Viewpoints vi
    Grounds for Dissent vi
    Red Team Critique vii
    MAGA Perspective viii
Page-by-Page Summaries ix
Notable Passages xvi

Abstracts

TL;DR (One Word)

Submarine development during WWI.

Explain It To Me Like I'm Five Years Old

During World War I, the United States Navy made changes to the way they built submarines. They talked a lot about how big the submarines should be, what kind of engines they should use, and what kind of weapons they should have. They also thought about how comfortable the sailors would be inside the submarines. They tried to make the submarines better by using new technology like listening devices, compasses that can tell which way they're going, underwater microphones, and radios. They did all this because they

TL;DR (Vanilla)

This document discusses the changes to US Navy submarine design during World War I, including size, propulsion systems, armament, and habitability. It highlights the efforts to improve technology and emphasizes the impact of the General Board on submarine development. Overall, it concludes that the Board's influence led to more capable submarines and future advancements.

Scientific Style

This document provides a comprehensive overview of the changes to United States Navy submarine design and construction during World War I. The focus is on the discussions and considerations of the Board regarding various aspects of submarine design, including size, propulsion systems, armament, and habitability systems. Efforts to improve submarine technology are highlighted, such as the use of listening devices, gyrocompasses, hydrophones, and radio sets. The impact of the General

Board of the US Navy on submarine design and development is emphasized, particularly in response to Germany's unrestricted submarine warfare. It is concluded that the Board's influence led to the development of more capable submarines, laying the foundation for future advancements.

ACTION ITEMS

Review the document to gain a comprehensive understanding of the changes to US Navy submarine design and construction during World War I.

Take note of the discussions and considerations of the Board regarding various aspects of submarine design, including size, propulsion systems, armament, and habitability systems.

Pay attention to the efforts made to improve submarine technology, such as the use of listening devices, gyrocompasses, hydrophones, and radio sets.

Analyze the impact of the General Board on submarine design and development in response to Germany's unrestricted submarine warfare.

Consider how the Board's influence affected the future of US submarine warfare.

VIEWPOINTS

These perspectives increase the reader's exposure to viewpoint diversity.

GROUNDS FOR DISSENT

One possible reason for a member of the organization responsible for this document to dissent from the report could be due to their belief that the Board's influence on submarine design and development was not as significant as claimed. They may argue that while the Board might have made some contributions, other factors such as technological advancements and lessons learned from previous conflicts played a more crucial role in shaping submarine design during World War I.

This dissenting member might argue that the document overlooks key technological advancements made by individuals or private companies outside of the Board's influence. They could point out specific examples where submarines were improved through innovations from independent engineers or companies, suggesting that it was not solely the Board's efforts that led to more capable submarines.

Additionally, this dissenting member might raise concerns about potential biases or limitations within the Board itself. They could argue that decision-making processes within the organization may have been influenced by political agendas, personal interests, or bureaucratic obstacles. By questioning the objectivity and integrity of the Board's decisions, they would undermine the report's conclusion that their influence had a positive impact on submarine development.

Moreover, this dissenter might criticize the document for its narrow focus on military effectiveness without adequately addressing ethical considerations. They might argue that unrestricted submarine warfare, which caused significant civilian casualties during World War I, should be seen as a negative consequence of the Board's influence rather than a commendable outcome. This principled objection would challenge the underlying assumption that any advancements in submarine technology are inherently positive.

Overall, a member of the organization responsible for this document may dissent due to their differing perspective on the significance of the

Board's influence, concerns about biases within the organization, and an emphasis on ethical considerations related to submarine warfare.

RED TEAM CRITIQUE

The document provides a comprehensive overview of United States Navy submarine design and construction during World War I. It covers various aspects such as size, propulsion systems, armament, and habitability systems, which shows a thorough analysis of the topic. The inclusion of efforts to improve submarine technology with listening devices, gyrocompasses, hydrophones, and radio sets demonstrates an understanding of the advancements made during that time.

However, there are several areas where this document could be improved. Firstly, it lacks specific examples or case studies to support its claims about the General Board's influence on submarine design and development. Without concrete evidence or references to specific submarines or technological advancements influenced by the Board's decisions, it is difficult to fully evaluate their impact.

Additionally, while the document mentions Germany's unrestricted submarine warfare as a catalyst for changes in US Navy submarine design and development in response to this threat; it fails to provide an adequate analysis of how these changes directly addressed Germany's tactics or countered them effectively. A deeper examination of the effectiveness of these changes in countering Germany's threats would strengthen the overall argument made in this document.

Furthermore, while there is mention of improvements made in submarine technology during World War I such as listening devices and hydrophones; no assessment is provided regarding their actual effectiveness or impact on submariner operations at that time. This lack of evaluation hinders our ability to understand how these advancements contributed significantly to creating more capable submarines.

In terms of structure and organization, the document could benefit from clearer section headings or subheadings that delineate different topics discussed within each aspect (size, propulsion systems). This would make it easier for readers to navigate through the information presented and understand each aspect being addressed more clearly.

Overall though providing a good general overview on United States Navy submarines' evolution during World War I with valuable insights into discussions held by the General Board; additional evidence supporting claims regarding their influence on specific designs or technologies along with assessing their effectiveness in countering German tactics would significantly strengthen the document's argument. In addition, incorporating a more detailed analysis of the impact of technological advancements on submarine capabilities and operations during that time period would enhance its comprehensiveness.

MAGA Perspective

Once again, we have a document that glorifies the decisions made by so-called experts in the US Navy. These bureaucrats who sit behind desks think they know better than the average American. They discuss and consider various aspects of submarine design as if they are the ones who will be risking their lives out on the open seas.

And what is this nonsense about improving technology? Listening devices, gyrocompasses, hydrophones, and radio sets? Who cares about all these fancy gadgets when our brave men are out there fighting for our freedoms? We need submarines that can effectively destroy our enemies, not submarines equipped with high-tech toys.

And let's not forget who we're talking about here - Germany. Yes, they were a threat during World War I, but why are we constantly playing catch-up to them? Instead of relying on the General Board of the US Navy to guide our submarine development, maybe we should take matters into our own hands and come up with innovative solutions that put us ahead of the game.

It's clear that this document is just another example of how our government bureaucracies waste taxpayer dollars. They pat themselves on the back for laying the foundation for future advancements, but at what cost? How much money was spent on these unnecessary discussions and considerations?

In the end, it's the American people who suffer. We should be focusing on strengthening our economy and protecting our borders, not wasting resources on naval innovations that may or may not make a difference in some far-off conflict. It's time to put America first and cut back on these wasteful projects.

PAGE-BY-PAGE SUMMARIES

BODY-1   *This page is a thesis on the changes made to United States Navy submarine design and construction during World War I, as determined by the General Board.*

BODY-2   *This page is a report on the changes made to United States Navy submarine design and construction during World War I, as determined by the General Board. It discusses the shift from defensive coastal roles to offensive deep ocean capabilities and aims to provide historical context for the development of naval technology.*

BODY-3   *The page is a thesis approval page for LCDR David R. Yocum, discussing changes to US Navy submarine design and construction during World War I.*

BODY-4   *This study examines the changes made to US Navy submarine design and construction during World War I, driven by the need to develop offensive capabilities in response to Germany's unrestricted submarine warfare. The General Board of the Navy played a key role in evaluating and implementing these changes. This research provides historical context for the development of naval technology and its influence on innovation in the interwar period.*

BODY-5   *The author expresses gratitude to their family, mentors, and ancestors for their support and inspiration in pursuing a study on naval history.*

BODY-6   *This page provides the table of contents for a thesis on German and US submarine development and employment during World War I, including chapters on submarine design and specifications.*

BODY-7   *The page contains the conclusion and bibliography of a document or book.*

BODY-8   *This page provides a list of acronyms related to naval warfare, including ASW, CARL, CNO, and SONAR.*

BODY-9   *The page contains two illustrations: one showing the U-117 submarine being turned over to Allied forces after the war, and another showing Electricians Mate Job Melvin Yocum on the bridge of the L-3.*

BODY-10   *The page contains various tables with size estimates and specifications for different submarine classes.*

BODY-11   *The U.S. Navy's view of submarines as offensive weapons changed during World War I due to the German Navy's use of submarines. This led to significant changes in submarine design and construction, overseen by the General Board of the Navy.*

BODY-12   *This page discusses the author's personal experience as a submarine officer and their interest in studying the changes to U.S. Navy submarine design and construction in response to German submarine use during World War I. The primary research question asks what changes were implemented or considered by the Board during this time period.*

BODY-13   *This page discusses the development of research questions and limitations for a study on changes to U.S. Navy submarine design and construction during World War I. It highlights the significance of understanding these changes in relation to modern naval challenges.*

BODY-14   *The literature review discusses the tactical use of submarines and changes to design during World War I. Primary sources, such as transcripts of Board hearings and autobiographies of Navy officers, provide detailed information on submarine design considerations and U.S. submarine usage during the war.*

BODY-15   *Various secondary literature sources, including books by Norman Friedman, George Baer, Eberhard Rossler, Brian Bond, Tim Benbow, and Gary E. Weir, provided*

BODY-16   *valuable insight into political influences on submarine design and the impact of U-Boat campaigns during World War I.*

BODY-16   *The page discusses the research design for studying submarine design and construction during World War I, including the factors that influenced changes in design and the role of the Board in directing these changes.*

BODY-17   *This page discusses the research methods and primary sources used in a thesis on the changes in submarine design and construction during World War I. It outlines the chapters of the thesis, including evaluations of German and British submarine development and the influence on the Board.*

BODY-18   *Germany developed and used submarines during World War I to counter the British blockade. They conducted two unrestricted submarine warfare campaigns, with the second leading to the United States joining the war. German submarine experimentation prior to the war resulted in improved engines.*

BODY-19   *The introduction of diesel engines in U-Boat designs during WWI significantly increased their range and offensive capabilities, allowing them to challenge British control of the sea.*

BODY-20   *The page discusses the threat posed by German U-Boats to British shipping during World War I and the failure of the patrol system to control them. It also mentions tactical features of U-Boat employment and the impact of Allied mining operations.*

BODY-21   *During World War I, the British Navy developed rapid diving procedures to counter U-Boat attacks. However, their efforts had little impact on shipping losses. This can be explained by the concept of disruptive innovation, where organizations cope effectively with innovations related to their primary mission but overlook those affecting secondary missions.*

BODY-22   *Germany's use of U-Boats and naval bases in Belgium allowed for the mass production and deployment of smaller, more efficient submarines during World War I. British intelligence identified the use of these submarines from Ostend and Zeebrugge, which required a vulnerable surface transit.*

BODY-23   *The sinking of the Lusitania led Germany to shift its strategy and focus on smaller submarines, which had significant impacts on the U.S. submarine design. These smaller submarines allowed Germany to continue to threaten Britain's maritime shipping and hinder their war efforts.*

BODY-24   *German U-Boats were used to lay minefields near British harbors during World War I.*

BODY-25   *During World War I, Germany used mine-laying submarines to attack important harbors on the British coast and later off the coast of the United States. The introduction of larger minelaying U-Boats, such as U-117, had a devastating impact on New England's coastline in August 1918. Lieutenant M.R. Pierce testified about German U-Boat construction, stating that by the end of March they had built 130 U-Boats.*

BODY-26   *Germany developed and modified the Ms-class U-Boats during World War I, increasing their offensive capability with additional torpedo tubes and larger guns. However, the focus shifted to smaller submarine types due to changes in submarine warfare tactics. German innovations were not limited to offense, as they also made advancements in atmospheric conditions within submarines.*

BODY-27   *The page provides information on the German UB-Boats during World War I, including their size estimates and the materials used in their control equipment. The* intelligence estimates were accurate for Class I and Class II, but began to diverge for Class III.

BODY-28   The page provides a table showing the size and classification of German U-boats during World War I. It also discusses the shift to larger UBII-class submarines and the need for an increased number of U-boats for naval operations.

BODY-29   The German Navy shifted focus to larger U-Boats during World War I, but also continued production of smaller submarines. Despite technological advantages, the U-Boat campaign ultimately failed due to the convoy system and lack of experienced submariners.

BODY-30   Germany's inability to maintain high levels of training for U-Boat crews during World War I resulted in increased losses and the failure of their Guerre de Course effort.

BODY-31   This chapter explores the evolution of U.S. and British submarine employment during World War I, including the shift from using submarines solely for defense to employing them in offensive tactics against German U-Boats.

BODY-32   In the early stages of World War I, submarines were initially used defensively. However, some naval officers recognized their potential threat to enemy fleets and merchant shipping. Others did not fully grasp the changing nature of warfare and the need for submarines in establishing control of the sea.

BODY-33   Germany's growing navy and the importance of fleet action in future wars took many by surprise. The US Navy initially discounted the importance of submarines but later increased their numbers for defensive use. Battleships and decisive naval action were still believed to be crucial.

BODY-34   The United States initially underestimated the threat of German submarines during World War I, but as they entered the war, they realized the severity of the situation. The Germans were inflicting significant damage to Allied supply ships, making submarines the gravest threat. Britain's vulnerability to economic warfare was also highlighted.

BODY 35   The page discusses the impact of Germany's unrestricted attacks on shipping during World War I, which led to a shortage of food and fuel in Great Britain. The convoy system was implemented to counter the threat of German submarines and minimize shipping losses.

BODY-36   During World War I, the convoy system was implemented for both inbound and outbound vessels to protect them from U-Boat attacks.

BODY-37   During World War I, the United States used submarines for offensive anti-submarine warfare operations off the coast of Ireland and in the Azores. The E, K, L, and O-class submarines were utilized for these missions, with specifications provided in the table.

BODY-38   Submarines were initially limited in their ability to operate far from support bases, but eventually became an effective weapon against German U-Boats during World War I. British submarines sank eleven U-Boats using torpedo attacks by August 1917.

BODY-39   During World War I, submarines played a crucial role in gathering covert information and patrolling American coasts. The E, N, and O-class submarines had different specifications in terms of displacement, length, speed, and armament.

BODY-40   Submariners in World War I recognized the importance of stealth and quick diving times. They operated with open valves on the surface to speed up the diving process. Maintaining high battery charge was crucial for underwater mobility, and firing multiple torpedoes required significant effort.

BODY-41 The page discusses the efforts to counter the German submarine force during World War I, including the use of the convoy system and various offensive strategies. The Board expressed frustration at the slow progress in implementing these measures due to infrastructure and tactical limitations.

BODY-42 Aircraft were being used to locate U-Boats and carry out attacks, while destroyers were found to be ineffective in close combat. The Board discussed expanding the submarine chaser program and developing listening technology.

BODY-43 The page discusses the recommendation to build 250 new chasers as part of an offensive campaign against submarines. It also mentions the use of mines as a possible solution and the British's efforts in mining the Heligoland Bight.

BODY-44 The page discusses the challenges of using mines and depth charges to combat U-Boats during winter months and suggests that closing the Straits of Dover would be an effective strategy. British submarines were found to be successful in countering U-Boats.

BODY-45 The page discusses the increasing importance of submarines in naval strategy during World War I and the technological developments that shaped their tactics. However, the impact of submarines was limited due to advancements in anti-submarine technology.

BODY-46 The page discusses the efforts made by the U.S. Navy to improve their design and tactics based on lessons learned from World War II and reverse engineering of captured U-Boats. It also mentions that the next chapter will focus on the design considerations for S-class and T-class submarines.

BODY-47 During World War I, the Board discussed submarine design based on German U-Boats and British designs. They focused on larger and more capable fleet submarines and considered various characteristics such as size, propulsion, endurance, speed, and hull characteristics.

BODY-48 Commander Boyd recommends smaller submarines similar to the British H-type for the U.S. antisubmarine effort, emphasizing the need for reliability and a large number of submarines.

BODY-49 The page discusses the recommendation for smaller submarines for coastal defense and submarine patrol, as well as their ability to conduct ASW. It also mentions the consideration of larger submarines for improved habitability.

BODY-50 The page discusses the importance of size and habitability in submarines during World War I, as well as the use of steam propulsion systems to achieve higher speeds.

BODY-51 The page discusses the design considerations and engine choices for U.S. submarines during World War I, including the use of steam and diesel engines. It also mentions the link between engine speed and detection ranges, highlighting the importance of maintaining a slow speed to avoid detection.

BODY-52 The page discusses the development of new U-cruisers with improved endurance and the establishment of submerged endurance requirements for U.S. submarines during a hearing in 1917. The goal was to achieve a submerged endurance of 100 nautical miles on a single charge.

BODY-53 The size of a submarine's motor and battery capacity determined its endurance, but the motor's impact on charging time posed a disadvantage. Reducing the battery size would sacrifice endurance, and lowering the minimum speed had limitations.

BODY-54 The page discusses the importance of speed in providing enough lifting force for a submarine to overcome negative buoyancy. It also highlights the need for sufficient supplies to increase human endurance on submarines.

BODY-55 The page discusses the speed requirements for submarines and the limitations of different propulsion systems. It also mentions discussions on the maximum submerged speed and the ability to operate at higher speeds at periscope depth.

BODY-56 British submarines were increasing their periscope depth and shear size to take advantage of increased pressure at deeper depths, allowing for higher speeds. Submerged speed of nine knots and sustainable battery capacity were important considerations.

BODY-57 The page discusses the depth specification and testing methods for submarines, as well as the decision to use single or double hull designs. It also mentions concerns about painting the hulls to reduce visibility and compartment specifications.

BODY-58 The page discusses the consideration of torpedo tube locations and the number of torpedoes to be carried in submarine designs. The use of broadside tubes is debated, with the British removing them from their designs. The consensus is that each tube should have a spare inboard for reloading.

BODY-59 The page discusses the selection of torpedo sizes and the consideration of building mine laying submarines during World War I. Some board members believed that smaller high-speed torpedoes and salvo launches would increase the likelihood of hitting enemy submarines, while others did not see a practical need for mine laying submarines at the time.

BODY-60 The page discusses the Board's consideration of mine laying submarines and the need for sufficient wet guns on future designs. It also mentions the development of hydrophones as a precursor to SONAR technology.

BODY-61 The page discusses the development of early listening devices on submarines during World War I, which allowed for the detection of submerged submarines. Initial installations were through the deck, but plans were made to install them through the hull. The performance and training of operators improved over time.

BODY-62 The page discusses the advancements in submarine detection technology during World War I, including the development of a superior hydrophone and the potential use of high frequency waves for locating submarines.

BODY-63 The page discusses the development of new hydrophone technology for detecting submarines, including a fish hydrophone and a towable hydrophone. These advancements allowed ships to detect submarines while remaining in motion, increasing their safety and effectiveness.

BODY-64 The page discusses the Mason apparatus and the K tube, which were used to locate submarines during World War I. These devices allowed for improved detection ranges and bearing resolution, and could be used in combination with other equipment to coordinate attacks on submarines.

BODY-65 The S-class submarines included gyrocompasses for navigation and British periscopes for situational awareness. To prevent friendly fire incidents, the use of lights as recognition signals was considered, and a high frequency pulse signaling device was proposed.

BODY-66 The page discusses the use of radio communication and habitability systems in submarines during World War I. It mentions the development of a secure signaling method for submarines and the use of radio sets with antennae. The habitability of submarines is also mentioned, with a focus on ventilation improvements.

BODY-67 US submarines in World War I lacked proper air-purification systems, causing poor air quality and health issues for personnel. British submarines were considered

BODY-68   *superior in ventilation. The US Navy obtained air-purifiers from the British to address the problem.*

BODY-68   *The "Gibbs" machine, a new air purifying equipment, was tested on submarines and proved to provide adequate breathing air. It consisted of a can of soda lime driven by a motor and was well-suited for confined spaces. The device required 10 cans for a 48-hour period.*

BODY-69   *Submarines required a supply of oxygen and a way to control hydrogen levels for extended submerged operations. Oxygen tanks were used to replenish the supply, while methods were discussed to filter and burn off excess hydrogen.*

BODY-70   *The page discusses methods for measuring and eliminating hydrogen on submarines, as well as efforts to handle carbon monoxide and chlorine gas.*

BODY-71   *The page discusses the importance of monitoring gas levels in submarines to ensure crew safety and extend the lifespan of equipment. It mentions specific recommendations for oxygen and carbon dioxide levels, as well as the development of devices to measure gas concentrations.*

BODY-72   *The page discusses the design considerations and specifications for the T-Class submarine during World War I. It includes recommendations for air purification apparatus and oxygen concentration levels onboard submarines.*

BODY-73   *Winterhalter inquired about starting work on a class of boats, but Land informed him that the current boats were being followed by contracted R-class and S-class boats. Land also presented a comparison of the S-class to the H-class, highlighting improvements and added equipment.*

BODY-74   *S-class submarines have numerous improvements over H-class submarines, including more torpedoes, the ability to carry a gun, better ventilation, additional equipment and amenities for the crew, and various technological advancements.*

BODY-75   *The U.S. H-Boats were considered better than the British K-Boats during the war, and efforts were made to secure a smaller design. However, progress was insufficient and contractors struggled to meet specifications. No new designs or construction were needed, just governmental pressure on private concerns and navy yard.*

BODY-76   *The Navy's approval of the S-class submarines ended the debate over building smaller submarines. The Board's efforts during World War I shifted control of submarine design to the Navy, allowing for technological development and influencing submarine development in World War II.*

BODY-77   *Germany's use of unrestricted submarine warfare during World War I prompted changes in naval thinking and tactics for the United States and Great Britain. This led to a shift towards smaller, more capable anti-submarine platforms such as destroyers and submarine chasers. The adoption of the convoy system proved successful in countering the German U-Boat threat.*

BODY-78   *Germany's shift in submarine usage during World War I influenced American naval officers to develop offensive submarine capability, leading to the production of smaller submarines for coastal operations.*

BODY-79   *The page discusses the shift from smaller U-Boats to larger submarines during World War II, influenced by German developments and the profit motives of US submarine manufacturers. Emory S. Land played a key role in advocating for larger submarines, which proved more capable in various operations. The page also highlights the technological advancements made during the war and the contributions of world-class scientists in developing submarine technology.*

BODY-80   The United States lacked in submarine technology, particularly in propulsion systems and mechanical equipment. Reverse engineering of captured German U-Boats helped close this gap. Further research is needed on submarine development, tactics, and doctrine during World War I, as well as the development of SONAR and atmospheric control equipment. The impact of the Board on submarine construction during World War I was significant.

BODY-81   The United States improved its submarine design by reverse engineering German U-Boats, allowing the Navy to control and direct future development. This led to successful advancements in U.S. submarines during the interwar period.

BODY-82   This page provides a bibliography of archival sources and books related to naval history, including topics such as sea power, submarine design, and the General Board of the US Navy.

BODY-83   A list of books and periodicals related to military strategy, naval operations, and shipbuilding in various time periods.

NOTABLE PASSAGES

BODY-4   "Germany's introduction of unrestricted submarine warfare forced the U.S. Navy to reevaluate the design of its submarines to develop an offensive deep ocean (blue water) capability."

BODY-5   "My chair, Dr. John T. Kuehn's assistance was nothing short of amazing as he helped guide and direct the work and research. He has shown me a love of naval history that is unparalleled."

BODY-11   "The subsequent reevaluation of the potential uses for submarines and their designs was driven by this new way of looking at the capabilities and advantages of a submarine platform. This re-evaluation led to significant changes in submarine design, construction, and use during the interwar period."

BODY-12   "My interest in this topic stems from my great grandfather, Job Melvin Yocum, having served on the submarine L-3 during World War I and my desire to learn more about the influence that war had on subsequent submarine design and construction."

BODY-13   With the increased challenges posed to today's naval forces by Chinese and Russian government Anti Access and Area Denial programs, it can be seen how submarine design and construction remains as important today as when Germany began its unrestricted submarine warfare campaign in World War I. Significant challenges drive changes in tactics and technology resulting in shifts in how submarines will be used in

BODY-19   "It was the diesel engine that changed the role of the German U-Boat from a defensive to an offensive one and made possible its successful application in a war of blockade."

BODY-20   "The German nation is basing its hope of victory on the success of the submarine."

BODY-21   "Some of the submarines take 2-1/2 minutes to submerge" and that "In that time we could cover about four miles."

BODY-23   "I find that the UC boats starting from UC-16 have 6,000 miles radius. The UB starting with 18 to UB-65 have 4500 miles. The U-boat radius starting with U-19 is 4250 miles and runs to 10,000 miles. There don't seem to be any diminution of the submarine menace as far as going through the North Sea [sic] is concerned."

BODY-25   "The fact is that they are placing mines at the mouths of practically every important harbor on the British Coast."

BODY-26   "The innovations implemented on these new U-Boats proved extremely effective in an offensive campaign but they had to wait until the resumption of unrestricted submarine warfare in 1917 to be fully realized."

BODY-28   "The shift away from unrestricted submarine warfare brought with it a shift to the slightly larger UBII-class starting in mid-1915. It was recognized that the UBI was inadequate with regard to range, battery, armament, periscopes, and communication masts. This bought about the UBII which incorporated all the desired improvements including the addition of another periscope and communication mast, and a 5-centimeter gun."

BODY-31   "Prior to World War I, the United States had employed submarines exclusively as a defensive weapon. Officers considered submarines best for coastal and harbor defense and they were kept close to their homeport."

BODY-32   "If the fleet were required to blockade Japan he thought the submarine in conjunction with mines and torpedoes constituted the greatest threat to the Navy."

BODY-33   "Our (Germany's) future is on the Sea."

BODY-34 "With America entering the war, the submarine situation off the British coast began to be understood by the United States. The Admiralty had been less than honest with the United States about the severity of the problem and the Navy was taken by surprise on receiving word from Admiral Sims in London regarding the severity of the threat facing Britain. As of October 1917, the Germans were inflicting a loss of 500,000 tons each month making the submarine the gravest threat to the Allies. The supply ships the Germans had been destroying were taking an enormous toll on the war effort."

BODY-35 "The reliance on the import of food combined with Germany's resumption of unrestricted attacks on shipping led Great Britain to the brink of starvation by 1917. It was estimated by October 1917 that Great Britain only had five months of flour and France only had one and a half months."

BODY-36 "It then became necessary to adopt the convoy system for outbound vessels also."

BODY-38 "During the last few months the British have come to the decision that submarines are one of the most important method for fighting German submarines."

BODY-39 "Submarines of the N and O-classes, as well as some of the E boats, patrolled American coasts and harbors following a defensive strategy."

BODY-40 "Wartime memoirs show almost an obsession with preserving the charge in the batteries, which was the only guarantee of a submarine's underwater mobility."

BODY-41 "The largest advances in tactics and naval warfare technology were centered around countering the German submarine force. It was recognized that the Germans had a relative superiority in their submarine design, in particular it was noted that their optics were significantly ahead of both the British and U.S. designs. This relative advantage was articulated by Pye when he said that the Germans 'undoubtedly sink more British boats than are lost by themselves.' The result was that multiple means had to be incorporated to counter the U-Boat threat."

BODY-42 "There was a growing desire to use aircraft for locating and cueing in surface vessels to execute an attack or to carry out a limited attack of their own."

BODY-44 "Captain F. H. Schofield, later to become a member of the Board and ultimately Commander-in-Chief Battle Force, told the Board that in his opinion the mining efforts were best used to close the Straits of Dover. Schofield felt that closing the Straights of Dover would result in a significant reduction in the sinking of merchant shipping."

BODY-45 "Many changes occurred during the war regarding the way a submarine should fit into a nation's naval strategy. The rising influence of the submarine could no longer be ignored and the future development and importance of the submarine to naval campaigns was just beginning to be understood. Ultimately, it was the changes in tactics facilitated by technological development that led to a continuing refinement of submarine employment and tactics."

BODY-48 "If the situation is such that a large number of submarines is needed and reliability was sought and that the Department was unwilling to try out any new device I should say a large number of small submarines of about the H-type of the British and our own would be advisable."

BODY-49 "We should be able to duplicate here anything abroad in submarines."

BODY-50 "A compromise had to be reached that could afford the smallest size possible while meeting the desire for improved habitability."

BODY-51 "A link between the engines and detection ranges with the newly developed listening devices like the C tube and the Mason apparatus was identified during the hearing on

13 November 1917. Captain R. H. Leigh, discussed how the G-1 could effectively avoid detection by running its engines at a lower revolution than the other submarines. Even though the G-1 was only able to maintain this reduced engine speed for eight minutes it did allow her to avoid detection during the reduced speed run."

BODY-52 "The desire was to achieve a submerged endurance of 100 nautical miles on a single charge resulting in the five knot for 20-hour requirement. The 100 nautical miles gave a submarine the ability to spend sufficient time submerged to avoid detection and if necessary open range from a counterattack."

BODY-53 "You have a motor for 9 knots and a battery for 5 knots for 20 hours. It will only deliver current at a certain rate. The current that motor will give as a generator will not be sufficient to charge that battery in the minimum time. You might have to take 10 or 12 hours. That is a decided disadvantage."

BODY-54 "It must also be recognized that diesel fuel storage and engine performance are only one component of endurance. The second component of endurance is human endurance. Sufficient stores must be brought onboard to feed and care for the crew."

BODY-55 "The only way to achieve speeds that high was to use steam turbine propulsion. The downside of a steam propulsion system being residual heat delaying submarine diving time to allow for cooling down the boiler."

BODY-56 "The combined effect being that as the submarine is then capable of a higher speed than at the shallower depth. Pierce explained how British submarines were shifting to a 30-foot periscope instead of a 25-foot periscope to take advantage of this concept. In conjunction with the longer periscope, British submarines were also shifting to a larger periscope shear in order to support the periscope."

BODY-57 "Retain positive buoyancy in a light condition with any compartment flooded."

BODY-60 "The Board was interested in ensuring sufficient wet guns on future designs. The concern was that by providing additional deck guns the speed would be affected. Early discussion was based on towing basin testing and it was noted by Commander T. A. Kearney 'the loss of speed was a little bigger than in actual service.' The Board was beginning to look at alternative mounting methods to increase the deck gun capacity and allow for two guns to include a 3-inch anti-aircraft gun."

BODY-61 "After initial demonstrations on submarine chasers there were experiments with installing them on submarines. The first installment went through the deck of the submarine in an arrangement that precluded use when the submarine was surfaced. Planning was begun for a means to install the sensor through the hull of the submarine allowing for use on the surface and when submerged."

BODY-62 "The continuing development of the new listening technology, toward what became SONAR, resulted in the development of a towable hydrophone, called the fish."

BODY-63 "The Admiralty feel that this fish hydrophone will be a great help in eliminating the submarine menace."

BODY-64 Leigh finished his discussion by detailing how he thought a combination of C tubes, K tubes and a triangle formation of multiple submarine chasers could be used to locate and maintain contact with a submarine to allow the chasers to coordinate an attack.

BODY-65 "While at periscope depth, nothing provides as much situational awareness as the periscope. Bingham had been impressed with the British periscopes during his visit to Europe and felt them to be superior to the optics employed on surfaces ships."

BODY-66 "The ventilation troubles can be easily straightened out . . . If they stayed out three days before they thought they."

BODY-67 "The air was quite bad, very bad, toward the end of the day and it was found necessary to start the air-purifiers going. The American boats are not equipped with those as they should be, and I suppose it is because the Americans have not considered it necessary to operate under water for so long a time as is now being done. The British have air-purifiers in all their boats. It consists of a motor which draws the air through chemicals."

BODY-68 "The 'Gibbs' machine consisted of a 40-pound can of soda lime driven by a one-quarter-horsepower motor that combined weighed 65-70 pounds."

BODY-69 "To facilitate extended submerged operations the submarines were fitted with tanks to hold compressed ... for seven days a boat needed 1,400 pounds of soda lime and 1,750 feet of oxygen with a net result that a submarine could operate 'free from the tender for a week and remain under 20 hours each day.'"

BODY-70 "Chlorine gas was the product of seawater interacting with an electric current, most notably occurring in the battery compartments."

BODY-71 "Never let oxygen fall below 17 percent and use a continuous bleed type delivery to avoid a mistake resulting in excessively low concentrations that could render the crew incapacitated."

BODY-72 "In this boat here, 2400 tons or more, 5 officers and 50 men, with a battery of two 5-inch guns, one 3-inch anti-aircraft gun, 21-inch torpedoes, four bow tubes and one 21-inch tube on each broadside, with the radius prescribed and stores for 45 days."

BODY-75 "No new designs are necessary. No new construction need be authorized. The problem is in hand. The one thing required is governmental pressure behind two private concerns and one navy yard."

BODY-76 "The efforts undertaken by the Board during the war led to the shift in control of submarine design away from the manufacturers and transferred it to the Navy. The Navy now having control over design prior to production allowed the Navy to dictate what technological development would be pursued as opposed to the manufacturers building a submarine without sufficient input from the submariners."

BODY-77 "No longer could the United States continue its Mahanian influenced buildup of battleships as the answer for achieving naval supremacy at sea. Smaller, more capable anti-submarine platforms came to dominate conventional U.S. naval construction during the war with the rise of the destroyer and the submarine chasers."

BODY-78 "The shift in thinking resulted in a conclusion that decisive battle was no longer a fleet on fleet battle as had been envisioned by Mahan—and especially his readers—but rather a U-Boat against a convoy escort force. The result being that continued effort over time protecting the lines of communication resulted in a cumulative victory that produced the same results as a decisive battle."

BODY-79 "The work done by these men laid the foundation of the interwar advances in SONAR, radio, atmospheric control equipment, navigation equipment, and more."

BODY-80 "German engineering had produced far superior submarines that were more reliable, longer lasting, and better performing than their American counterparts. It took reverse engineering of the captured and surrendered U-Boats during the early interwar period to allow the United States to finally close this gap."

BODY-81 "The combined efforts of the Board and key submariners such as Emery S. Land led to a hugely successful interwar advancement of U.S. submarines."

CHANGES TO UNITED STATES NAVY SUBMARINE DESIGN
AND CONSTRUCTION DURING WORLD WAR I, AS
DETERMINED BY THE GENERAL BOARD

A thesis presented to the Faculty of the U.S. Army
Command and General Staff College in partial
fulfillment of the requirements for the
degree

MASTER OF MILITARY ART AND SCIENCE
Military History

by

DAVID R. YOCUM, LCDR, U.S. NAVY
B.S., University of New Mexico, Albuquerque, New Mexico, 2006

Fort Leavenworth, Kansas
2017

Approved for public release; distribution is unlimited. Fair use determination or copyright permission has been obtained for the inclusion of pictures, maps, graphics, and any other works incorporated into this manuscript. A work of the United States Government is not subject to copyright, however further publication or sale of copyrighted images is not permissible.

REPORT DOCUMENTATION PAGE		Form Approved OMB No. 0704-0188
Public reporting burden for this collection of information is estimated to average 1 hour per response, including the time for reviewing instructions, searching existing data sources, gathering and maintaining the data needed, and completing and reviewing this collection of information. Send comments regarding this burden estimate or any other aspect of this collection of information, including suggestions for reducing this burden to Department of Defense, Washington Headquarters Services, Directorate for Information Operations and Reports (0704-0188), 1215 Jefferson Davis Highway, Suite 1204, Arlington, VA 22202-4302. Respondents should be aware that notwithstanding any other provision of law, no person shall be subject to any penalty for failing to comply with a collection of information if it does not display a currently valid OMB control number. **PLEASE DO NOT RETURN YOUR FORM TO THE ABOVE ADDRESS.**		

1. REPORT DATE (DD-MM-YYYY) 09-06-2017	2. REPORT TYPE Master's Thesis	3. DATES COVERED (From - To) AUG 2016 – JUN 2017
4. TITLE AND SUBTITLE Changes to United States Navy Submarine Design and Construction during World War I, as Determined by the General Board		5a. CONTRACT NUMBER
		5b. GRANT NUMBER
		5c. PROGRAM ELEMENT NUMBER
6. AUTHOR(S) LCDR David R. Yocum, U.S. Navy		5d. PROJECT NUMBER
		5e. TASK NUMBER
		5f. WORK UNIT NUMBER
7. PERFORMING ORGANIZATION NAME(S) AND ADDRESS(ES) U.S. Army Command and General Staff College ATTN: ATZL-SWD-GD Fort Leavenworth, KS 66027-2301		8. PERFORMING ORG REPORT NUMBER
9. SPONSORING / MONITORING AGENCY NAME(S) AND ADDRESS(ES)		10. SPONSOR/MONITOR'S ACRONYM(S)
		11. SPONSOR/MONITOR'S REPORT NUMBER(S)

12. DISTRIBUTION / AVAILABILITY STATEMENT
Approved for Public Release; Distribution is Unlimited

13. SUPPLEMENTARY NOTES

14. ABSTRACT
Prior to World War I, the United States envisioned employing submarines in a defensive role for coastal and harbor defense. Submarines' defensive role was based on the current state of U.S. submarine technology making long range open ocean operations difficult. Germany's introduction of unrestricted submarine warfare forced the U.S. Navy to reevaluate the design of its submarines to develop an offensive deep ocean (blue water) capability. The work for redesigning submarines, while carried out by contractors, was initiated by the actions of the General Board of the Navy, the primary military advisory committee to the Secretary of the Navy for all matters concerning naval operations, war plans, and responsibility for determining requirements for naval ships. As the primary driver for change, the Board evaluated current designs against evolving requirements to determine the best course for future design development. The Boards' official transcripts provide detailed information regarding the considerations affecting changes to designs made during the war to understand the changes implemented. Much academic work has been devoted to the development of submarines during the interwar period, however, very little is available regarding changes initiated during the war. This study addresses the question of what changes came about during the war and the final state of submarine construction and design at the end of the war with the goal of providing historical context regarding development of naval technology and influence of operational doctrine that led to significant innovation during the interwar period.

15. SUBJECT TERMS
Anti-Submarine Warfare (ASW), Convoy, General Board, Submarine, U-Boat, World War I

16. SECURITY CLASSIFICATION OF:			17. LIMITATION OF ABSTRACT	18. NUMBER OF PAGES	19a. NAME OF RESPONSIBLE PERSON
a. REPORT (U)	b. ABSTRACT (U)	c. THIS PAGE (U)	(U)	83	19b. PHONE NUMBER (include area code)

Standard Form 298 (Rev. 8-98)
Prescribed by ANSI Std. Z39.18

MASTER OF MILITARY ART AND SCIENCE

THESIS APPROVAL PAGE

Name of Candidate: LCDR David R. Yocum

Thesis Title: Changes to United States Navy submarine design and construction during World War I, as determined by the General Board

Approved by:

_____, Thesis Committee Chair
John T. Kuehn, Ph.D.

_____, Member
Harold A. Laurence, Ph.D.

_____, Member
CDR David Stebbins, M.S.

Accepted this 9th day of June 2017 by:

_____, Director, Graduate Degree Programs
Prisco R. Hernandez, Ph.D.

The opinions and conclusions expressed herein are those of the student author and do not necessarily represent the views of the U.S. Army Command and General Staff College or any other governmental agency. (References to this study should include the foregoing statement.)

ABSTRACT

CHANGES TO UNITED STATES NAVY SUBMARINE DESIGN AND CONSTRUCTION DURING WORLD WAR I, AS DETERMINED BY THE GENERAL BOARD, by LCDR David R. Yocum, 83 pages.

Prior to World War I, the United States envisioned employing submarines in a defensive role for coastal and harbor defense. Submarines' defensive role was based on the current state of U.S. submarine technology making long range open ocean operations difficult. Germany's introduction of unrestricted submarine warfare forced the U.S. Navy to reevaluate the design of its submarines to develop an offensive deep ocean (blue water) capability. The work for redesigning submarines, while carried out by contractors, was initiated by the actions of the General Board of the Navy, the primary military advisory committee to the Secretary of the Navy for all matters concerning naval operations, war plans, and responsibility for determining requirements for naval ships. As the primary driver for change, the Board evaluated current designs against evolving requirements to determine the best course for future design development. The Boards' official transcripts provide detailed information regarding the considerations affecting changes to designs made during the war to understand the changes implemented.

Much academic work has been devoted to the development of submarines during the interwar period, however, very little is available regarding changes initiated during the war. This study addresses the question of what changes came about during the war and the final state of submarine construction and design at the end of the war with the goal of providing historical context regarding development of naval technology and influence of operational doctrine that led to significant innovation during the interwar period.

ACKNOWLEDGMENTS

Many people have assisted me in this endeavor; without their help and support none of this would have been possible. My wife, Stacie, and my children, Madison, Elijah, and Charlie, all helped more than they know by supporting and encouraging me. My chair, Dr. John T. Kuehn's assistance was nothing short of amazing as he helped guide and direct the work and research. He has shown me a love of naval history that is unparalleled. Dr. Harold A. Laurence and CDR David .L Stebbins helped tremendously by providing feedback and encouragement that helped me stay the course and grow in the process. My parents and grandparents and the constant support and the love of country they imparted to me will never be forgotten. And finally, my great grandfather, a World War I submariner for giving me the inspiration to pursue this course of study. This work is for all of you.

TABLE OF CONTENTS

Page

MASTER OF MILITARY ART AND SCIENCE THESIS APPROVAL PAGE iii

ABSTRACT.. iv

ACKNOWLEDGMENTS v

TABLE OF CONTENTS.. vi

ACRONYMS viii

ILLUSTRATIONS ix

TABLES x

CHAPTER 1 INTRODUCTION 1

    Background 1
    Research Questions... 2
    Limitations and Delimitations 3
    Significance 3
    Literature Review 4
    Research Design 6

CHAPTER 2 GERMAN SUBMARINE DEVELOPMENT AND EMPLOYMENT 8

CHAPTER 3 U.S. SUBMARINE EMPLOYMENT...21

CHAPTER 4 EVOLUTION OF SUBMARINE DESIGN, 1916-1918 37

    Size Considerations... 38
    Propulsion Systems 40
    Endurance 42
    Speed and Depth Considerations 45
    Hull Characteristics.. 47
    Primary Armament 48
    Secondary Armament 50
    Sensor Systems 50
    Navigation and Signals Equipment... 55
    Habitability Systems 56
    Consolidated Specification Summary... 62

CHAPTER 5 CONCLUSIONS 67

BIBLIOGRAPHY 72

ACRONYMS

ASW	Anti-Submarine Warfare
CARL	Combined Arms Research Library
CNO	Chief of Naval Operations
SONAR	Sound Navigation and Ranging

ILLUSTRATIONS

                                                                                                                            Page

Figure 1. U-117 with U.S. Sailor following Turnover to Allied Forces after the War.....14

Figure 2. Electricians Mate Job Melvin Yocum on the Bridge of the L-3 26

TABLES

                                                                                 Page

Table 1. UB-class Size Estimates 17

Table 2. UB-class Size Actual 18

Table 3. Specifications for E, K, L, and O-class Submarines 27

Table 4. Specifications for E, N, and O-class Submarines 29

Table 5. S-class Improvements over H-class 64

CHAPTER 1

INTRODUCTION

Background

Prior to World War I, the U.S. Navy did not view the submarine as an offensive weapon. The Secretary of the Navy, Josephus Daniels, as late as June of 1915, still believed that submarines were best utilized for harbor defense.[1] The usage of the submarine as an offensive weapon by the German Navy during the war caused the U.S. Navy to reevaluate its future use of the submarine. The subsequent reevaluation of the potential uses for submarines and their designs was driven by this new way of looking at the capabilities and advantages of a submarine platform. This re-evaluation led to significant changes in submarine design, construction, and use during the interwar period. The primary agent for determining changes to ship construction and design was the influential General Board of the Navy. Under the direction of Admiral of the Navy George Dewey and his successors, the Board oversaw the effort to understand the novel ways Germany employed the submarine and the best ways to counter this new usage, to say nothing of its use as part of a sea going battle fleet. It also oversaw the efforts to change the U.S. Navy submarine design and construction.

Prevailing beliefs about submarine usage in war leading up to World War I led the United States to adopt a much less offensive design and employment concept for submarines. The concept of naval power at the time was inextricably linked to battleships and the ideas of Captain A. T. Mahan. Many leaders within the Navy failed to recognize

---

[1] Josephus Daniels, *The Cabinet Diaries of Josephus Daniels, 1913-1921,* ed. David Cronon (Lincoln: University of Nebraska Press, 1963), 101.

that a naval war could occur entirely without full fleet engagement and thus require the novel use of lesser known and used vessels within a naval arsenal.

Serving as a submarine officer for the last ten years and as an enlisted submariner the previous six, I have been onboard three U.S. submarines during major construction and modernization periods. While an enlisted Engineering Laboratory Technician onboard the USS *Ohio* (SSGN-726), I experienced the beginning of the SSGN conversion process. After commissioning and follow on training I served onboard USS *Texas* (SSN-775) for the completion of her Post Shakedown Availability as well as the subsequent modernization of her sonar, fire control and navigation systems. I served most recently as the Combat Systems Officer onboard USS *Seawolf* (SSN-21) where I completed two Northern Atlantic deployments and oversaw the commencement of her Engineering Department Selected Restricted Availability and modernization of her sonar, fire control, and navigation systems. My interest in this topic stems from my great grandfather, Job Melvin Yocum, having served on the submarine *L-3* during World War I and my desire to learn more about the influence that war had on subsequent submarine design and construction.

Research Questions

This study will examine the changes to U.S. Navy submarine design and construction in response to the German use of submarines during World War I. The primary research question asks: what changes to submarine design and construction were implemented or considered by the Board during World War I? It also explores and searches for the specific driving factors of change for the U.S. Navy in submarine design and construction from 1914 to 1918. The primary research question drove the development of several secondary research questions: (1) what specifically was determined to be the factors of change to the U.S. Navy submarine design and construction; (2) what changes to submarine design and construction were mandated by the Board during World War I; (3) who were the primary proponents for changes to submarine design and construction within the Board; (4) what inputs for conceptual design changes were considered by the Board; and (5) what does the existing literature say about the primary question?

Limitations and Delimitations

This thesis is limited to primary source material from the Combined Arms Research Library (CARL) and the National Archives as available online, via email contacts, or Dr. Kuehn's collection of archival material will be used for this study. The study assumes that little to no travel money or time will be available to conduct the research. The serials of the Board were inaccessible; therefore the research was limited to the hearings of the Board. This study will be delimited to U.S. submarine construction and design changes brought about by World War I. The study will look at documents from 1914 to 1918 as well as published studies tangent and pertinent to the topic.

Significance

With the increased challenges posed to today's naval forces by Chinese and Russian government Anti Access and Area Denial programs, it can be seen how submarine design and construction remains as important today as when Germany began its unrestricted submarine warfare campaign in World War I. Significant challenges drive changes in tactics and technology resulting in shifts in how submarines will be used in the future and likewise, changes in how a submarine is used will result in further changes to design and technology.

Literature Review

Much literature exists that discusses the tactical use of submarines and the official Navy position regarding submarines prior to and during World War I. Secondary sources regarding changes to design during World War I have very little information but provided context and background information about the changes to usage during the war that led to changes in design and construction. Primary source and archival information is more detailed regarding submarine design and changes considered during the war.

The archived records of the Board were the largest information source for this study. Transcripts of the Board hearings provide detailed information about submarine design considerations evaluated during World War I and describe actions taken by the Board.

The research also included several other published primary sources. The autobiography of Rear Admiral Bradley A. Fisk, *From Midshipman to Rear-Admiral*, and biography of Rear Admiral Stephen B. Luce by Rear Admiral Albert Gleaves, *Life and Letters of Rear Admiral Stephen B. Luce*, provided the thoughts of senior U.S. Navy officers on the eve of World War I regarding U.S. submarine usage and Germany's use of unrestricted submarine warfare. *The Cabinet Diaries of Josephus Daniels 1913-1921*, Secretary of the Navy during the Wilson administration, provided the viewpoints of the cabinet and the Wilson administration regarding the submarine threat as well as interactions between the Secretary of the Navy and the Board. All of these sources provided valuable insight into the political influences on the Board and submarine design in general.

Several secondary literature sources were also extremely informative. The book by Norman Friedman, *Submarine Design and Development* (1984), provided an overview of submarine development leading up to World War I as well as a brief analysis of submarine usage by the German, British, and U.S. navies during the war. Friedman's book, however, focuses primarily on the interwar period and is largely silent on any changes considered during World War I itself. George Baer's book, *One Hundred Years of Sea Power* (1994), provided a good analysis of the political situation in the U.S. leading up to and during World War I. His analysis provided much needed context to understand the influences on the Navy in preparation for and execution of the war. Eberhard Rossler's book, *The U-boat: The Evolution and Technical History of German Submarines,* translated by Harold Erenberg (1975), provided a detailed look at U-Boat development both prior to and during the war. Rossler's book allowed for a comparison of U.S. and British intelligence estimates discussed in the Board's records and provided relevant background to the tactics employed by Germany during the war.

Brian Bond's *Britain's Two World Wars Against Germany, Myth, Memory and the Distortions of Hindsight,* (2014) provided details of the effect of the German U-Boat campaigns on Great Britain. Tim Benbow's review of Gautama Makunda's, *We Cannot Go On: Disruptive Innovation and the First World War Royal Navy* (2010), provided background about the failure of the Royal Navy to counter the U-Boat threat to merchant shipping. The most useful secondary source used for this study was Gary E. Weir's book *Building American Submarines, 1914-1940* (1991). Weir's analysis of the processes in place for submarine construction and design in the period just prior to World War I and discussion of the factors influencing design during the war were extremely useful. Specifically, his work identified the contractor led research and development process used during this time that resulted in submarines that were technologically inferior to the German U-Boats employed during the war. The article "Josephus Daniels and the U.S. Navy's Shipbuilding Program During World War I" (1996), by William Williams provided additional background on the driving factors behind the Navy's overall construction program.

Research Design

There was sufficient literature on submarines during World War I, however, much of it was limited to the tactical adaptation required by the allied navies to overcome Germany's use of unrestricted submarine warfare. This study focuses on those sources that provided background information regarding German and U.S. submarine design and construction and the tactical considerations that drove change. Additionally, the shift in U.S. interests leading to more control of the design and constructions of submarines by the Board will be evaluated to include the factors that led to this shift. Finally, the tactical and design changes that resulted during World War I will be researched.

The transcripts of the Board starting in 1917 were available at the CARL. Dr. Kuehn also provided scanned copies of various correspondence of the Board. These documents were all used to determine what changes the Board directed for submarine design and construction from 1914 to 1918.

The specific characteristics of submarine design that were addressed by the Board directly and those that were evaluated by industry will be researched. The considerations leading to the Board assuming more power in the design and construction of submarines will also be researched to determine what factors led to increased Navy involvement in control of submarine design.

Primary sources, primarily the microfilm *Proceedings and Hearings of the General Board* at CARL will be used to determine what changes were made to submarine construction and design as a result of World War I. Contemporary journals such as the U.S. Naval Institute *Proceedings* may also be used to assess the attitudes of naval officers of the periods. Dr. Kuehn has made some Board studies material available as well. Several additional primary sources, specifically the Cabinet Diaries of Josephus Daniels will be used to determine inputs to the Board regarding submarine construction and design change requirements.

This thesis consists of five chapters. Chapter 1 reviewed the thesis purpose, scope, research questions, and literature review. Chapter 2 is an evaluation of German submarine development, both technological advances and tactical usage, prior to and during the war. Chapter 3 evaluates the tactical use of the submarine by Great Britain and the United States and the approach taken by both nations to counter the U-Boat. Additionally, chapter 3 will assess the influence the technological advances and changing tactics had on the Board during the war. Chapter 4 will be a review of the hearings of the Board, regarding submarine design and construction changes considered or implemented during World War I. Chapter 5 will be a summary and conclusion of influences on and changes to U.S. submarine design and construction and a discussion of areas requiring further study.

CHAPTER 2

GERMAN SUBMARINE DEVELOPMENT AND EMPLOYMENT

The German employment of the U-Boat during World War I developed as a means to counter the British blockade of Germany and the inability of the German Navy's High Seas Fleet to counter the Royal Navy's Grand Fleet at sea. Germany conducted two separate unrestricted submarine warfare periods during the war. The first campaign began on 4 February 1915 with the German declaration of the submarine campaign and the warning that neutral shipping was at risk due to the "difficulties of clear identification."[2] This first campaign was ultimately abandoned due to fears that it would draw the United States into the war. Following the Battle of Jutland on 31 May 1916, the German fleet did not sail again as a consolidated fleet for the remainder of the war. Therefore, to counter the British threat, Germany turned to the submarine as the best way to continue to fight the blockade of their ports and the second campaign began on 9 January 1917 after the Kaiser issued a new declaration of unrestricted submarine warfare. The interception of a letter sent by Germany to Mexico asking them to declare war against the United States, the infamous Zimmerman note, and the resumption of unrestricted warfare drove the United states to finally join the war on 6 April 1917.[3]

German submarine experimentation prior to the war, starting in 1904, resulted in the older paraffin burning engines being replaced by the more powerful and reliable

---

[2] Daniels, 29 June 1915, 97 (notes).

[3] Eberhard Rossler, *The U-boat: The Evolution and Technical History of German Submarines,* trans. Harold Erenbert (Annapolis, MD: Naval Institute Press, 1975), 75.

diesel engines in U-Boat designs by the end of 1910.[4] This change resulted in several significant improvements. First it allowed for a significantly increased range over the paraffin engines and second it burned much cleaner in that it did not produce the thick white smoke associated with burning paraffin. It was through the introduction of the diesel engine that the true capability of the U-Boats as a commerce raider was finally recognized. A noted German historian, Eberhard Rossler wrote, "It was the diesel engine that changed the role of the German U-Boat from a defensive to an offensive one and made possible its successful application in a war of blockade."[5] The extended range afforded by the new diesel engine allowed U-Boats to attack British shipping not only in the English Channel but to expand into the western approaches to the British Isles. The recognition of the possibilities provided by this increased range, combined with the inability of the German fleet to directly challenge the British at sea, led to the primary influence of the U-Boat during the remainder of the war as a Guerre de Course weapon. According to Rossler, "Tirpitz had placed little trust in U-boats, but as the war progressed he had become strongly convinced of their indispensable role."[6]

With the ability to send a U-Boat not just into the channel but to be able to send them to the west of Ireland allowed the Germans to hazard British shipping commencing a Guerre de Course that eventually challenged the British control of the sea despite the lack of further decisive surface battles. The British estimated that there were up to five submarines going through the English Channel each day and this presented a serious

---

[4] Rossler, 25-28.

[5] Ibid., 31.

[6] Ibid., 53.

challenge to the Royal Navy.[7] As was stated by the Board, the U-Boats were destroying shipping at a rate of 500,000 tons each month. With such a high rate of loss, the Board thought it would take until October 1918 to generate the ship building capacity required to exceed the loss rate. In effect as the Board noted "The German nation is basing its hope of victory on the success of the submarine."[8] The British had been attempting to control the U-Boat problem by using a patrol system to locate and destroy the German submarines. Commander Taussig discussed the failure of the patrol system to limit U-Boat sinking of British shipping, and how in the two weeks prior to his ship's arrival, the British had lost 95 ships.[9] This is discussed further in chapter 3. This type of success by the U-Boats against allied shipping was routine until the convoy system was adopted.

Several tactical features of German U-Boat employment were identified by British and subsequently American naval intelligence. It was noted that German commanders were very navigation conscious and routinely fixed their position. The U-Boats were also known to submerge when they sighted a destroyer. It was also identified that the Allied mining operations were having an effect since the U-Boats were now having to go "around the tip of Jutland" to get around the channel and that the German Navy was increasing the use of mine sweepers to clear a path for their U-Boats to get to

---

[7] *Proceedings and Hearings of the General Board of the US Navy, 1900-1950*, vol. 1-2, 14 August-31 December 1918, Archival Information Record Group 80, Combined Arms Research Library, Fort Leavenworth, KS, (microfilm), 137. Hereafter referred to as PHGB.

[8] PHGB, 1917, 420.

[9] Ibid., 686.

sea.[10] In order to press an attack, it was assumed the U-Boat had to surface to be able to fire a torpedo. While executing an attack the U-Boat was vulnerable to counter-attack and therefore submerged once it had been fired upon.[11] The need for rapid diving procedures developed during the war as the British began to target the U-Boats with aircraft. It was noted by Lieutenant Commander Davis of the Royal Naval Air Service that "Some of the submarines take 2-1/2 minutes to submerge" and that "In that time we could cover about four miles."[12] This suggests the importance of stealth for a submarine and highlighting the necessity to be submerged during daylight to prevent being spotted by an aircraft. The British Navy was able to take advantage of this information and were successful in using the destroyers they did have to control the U-Boat threat against the Grand Fleet but the Royal Navy's efforts had little impact on the losses to shipping. The stark contrast between the response to one and the lack thereof with the other has been explained by Tim Benbow's review of Gautam Makunda's theory of disruptive innovation. They explain the effects of disruptive innovation on an organization in relation to its primary mission and secondary missions. "Those impacting the company's primary mission, or 'sustaining innovations,' tend to be coped with highly effectively but those affecting secondary missions can be overlooked."[13] Makunda uses this disruptive innovation concept to explain why the Royal Navy was able to successfully counter the U-Boat

---

[10] PHGB, 1917, 457.

[11] Ibid., 690.

[12] Ibid., 678.

[13] Tim Benbow, "We Cannot Go On: Disruptive Innovation and the First World War Royal Navy," *Security Studies* 19, no. 1 (January 2010): 124-159

threat to the Grand Fleet but failed to adapt to the German use of the U-Boat against merchant shipping.

One additional consideration that significantly aided the German Navy in employing the new diesel U-Boats was the establishment of naval bases in Belgium. By moving the submarines forward, they were able to take advantage of the new technology and mass-produce many smaller U-Boats to use from the forward bases. German construction of the UB-classes began in late 1914 with the intentions of building a U-Boat that was rail portable to facilitate a rapid deployment to forward ports for assembly and use. Based on the constraints of a rail portable U-Boat, the final UB design was roughly 125 tons with a 60-horsepower diesel and a 120-horsepower motor with a battery that provided ten hours at four knots and allow for a maximum speed of 5.5 knots submerged and a 1,600-mile surface range. Similarly, the UC was built to be a rail portable U-Boat based on a UB-class design modified to carry 12 mines.[14] British intelligence assessed that UB and UC-class boats were being employed from Ostend and Zeebrugge on the Belgian coast. The use of Ostend and Zeebrugge required a long surface transit of between fifteen and twenty miles during which time the U-Boats were more vulnerable.[15]

Following the initial success of the UB and UC-class U-Boats, Germany developed slightly larger designs of both classes during 1915. Both new classes were no longer rail portable but had significantly improved endurance ranges based on a larger displacement allowing more storage space for fuel. Several incidents including the

---

[14] Rossler, 40-41.

[15] PHGB, 1917, 457.

sinking of the *Lusitania* in 1915 resulted in Germany shifting its strategy from unrestricted submarine warfare to keep the United States from entering the war. The shift in policy, along with the realization that the war would last much longer than anticipated, led Germany to focus on the UCII-class minelaying submarine.[16]

The introduction of smaller German submarines had significant impacts on the Board during its deliberations regarding the future U.S. submarine design. The utility of the smaller German submarines was that Germany could produce a significant number of submarines to replace wartime losses that larger submarines did not allow. The Board's assessment of the U-boat endurance as of 19 October 1917 was stated by the former Commander-in-Chief of the Atlantic Fleet, Admiral Albert Winterhalter: "I find that the UC boats starting from UC-16 have 6,000 miles radius. The UB starting with 18 to UB-65 have 4500 miles. The U-boat radius starting with U-19 is 4250 miles and runs to 10,000 miles. There don't seem to be any diminution of the submarine menace as far as going through the North Sea [sic] is concerned."[17] Despite not having the full range of the fleet submarines, these smaller U-Boats based forward allowed the Germans to continue to hold Great Britain's maritime shipping at risk and hinder Britain's war efforts on the continent.

---

[16] Rossler, 52-53.

[17] PHGB, 1917, 497.

Figure 1. U-117 with U.S. Sailor following Turnover
to Allied Forces after the War

Source: From author's personal collection.

Another significant use for the German U-Boats was found in laying minefields in vicinity of the entrances to British harbors. Starting early in 1915, Germany began planning for their UE-class that was to be between 600 and 700 tons and provide dry storage for 34 mines.[18] According to Mr. C. E. Eveleth, who was working on the listening technology and had just come back from Europe, "The fact is that they are placing mines at the mouths of practically every important harbor on the British Coast."[19] The successful employment of these mine-laying submarines forced the British to significantly increase the number of mine sweepers and patrol vessels.[20] This effort was extended to include mining operations off the coast of the United States later in the war with the introduction of a larger minelaying U-Boat. U-117 was the first of the larger mine laying U-Boats and with a displacement of 1,164 tons she was more than twice as large as the UCIII-class and with a range of 12,500 nautical miles could reach the United States.[21] The U-117 had a devastating impact off the New England coastline in August of 1918. During her attacks along the coast from Cape Hatteras to Long Island, she sank five vessels directly, four by mines and damaged one additional ship with a mine. During her return transit, she sank an additional five vessels.[22]

Lieutenant M. R. Pierce testified about the estimated status of German U-Boat construction during his hearing with the Board on 9 October 1917. Pierce described how the Germans had three different types of submarines and that as of the end of March they had built 130 U-Boats. The U-Boats were believed to be a double hull boat of

---

[18] Rossler, 45.

[19] PHGB, 1918, 137.

[20] Ibid., 1917, 418.

[21] Rossler, 332.

[22] Gary E. Weir, *Building American Submarines, 1914-1940* (Washington, DC: Naval Historical Center, Department of the Navy, 1991), 10.

approximately 700 tons.[23] This type was the current Ms-class that the Germans had estimated in 1915 that they needed at least 48 of to execute the blockade of Great Britain. Germany had slightly reduced the tonnage to be 600-650 tons thereby making production faster to make up for wartime losses. Germany ordered 11 additional Ms-class on 16 June 1915 to expand its offensive capability. The new modified Ms-class was designed with four bow torpedo tubes and two stern tubes and had a sharper bow to cut through the submarine nets. The senior member of the Board, Admiral Charles Badger, mentioned during the 4 December 1917 hearing on anti-submarine warfare that it had been assessed the Germans were using a 5.9-inch gun on their newer U-Boats.[24] This intelligence turned out to be accurate since a 15-centimeter gun was mounted on the Large Ms U-Boat, the Large Minelaying U-Boat and two 15-centimeter guns were mounted on the U-cruisers.[25] The cessation of unrestricted submarine warfare by the autumn of 1915 shifted the focus from this type to the smaller UBII and UCII type.[26] The innovations implemented on these new U-Boats proved extremely effective in an offensive campaign but they had to wait until the resumption of unrestricted submarine warfare in 1917 to be fully realized.

German innovations during this time were by no means limited to offensive capability. Mr. E. S. Land, the naval constructor, a future vice admiral and Chief of the Bureau of Construction and repair, described to the Board how German atmospheric

---

[23] PHGB, 1917, 353.

[24] Ibid., 691.

[25] Rossler, 331-332.

[26] Ibid., 48-50.

control equipment was very similar to the American design but that their "Draeger apparatus" used potassium hydroxide vice the soda lime the U.S. device used. It was not assessed to be superior to the U.S. soda lime and there was thought that the Germans might even be shifting to the soda lime due to shortage of potash caused by explosives production.[27]

Land laid out for the Board on 14 April 1918 the current estimate of the relative size of the UB-Boats. Table 1 is taken from his hearing before the Board.

Table 1. UB-class Size Estimates

Class I	No. 1 to 17	125 tons
Class II	No. 18 to 47	250 tons
Class III	No. 48 to 72	700 tons
Class III	No. 72 to 100 and upwards	At least 700 tons and probably 800, as their length is[sic] 213 feet and they more nearly approach the double hull sea-going U-Boat.

Source: Created by author using data from *Proceedings and Hearings of the General Board of the US Navy, 1900-1950,* vol. 1-2, 14 August-31 December 1918, Archival Information Record Group 80, Combined Arms Research Library, Fort Leavenworth, KS, (microfilm), 539.

As can be seen by comparing the above table with the actual displacements of the UB-classes the intelligence estimates were remarkably accurate with regard to Class I and Class II however they began to diverge beginning with Class III. The actual displacements are in table 2.

---

[27] PHGB, 1917, 650.

Table 2.   UB-class Size Actual

Class I	No. 1 to 17	127 tons
Class II	No. 18 to 47	263 tons
Class III	No. 48 to 72	516 tons
Class III	No. 72 to 100 and upwards	516 tons

Source: Created by author using data from Eberhard Rossler, *The U-boat: The Evolution and Technical History of German Submarines,* trans. Harold Erenbert (Annapolis, MD: Naval Institute Press, 1975), 332.

The shift away from unrestricted submarine warfare brought with it a shift to the slightly larger UBII-class starting in mid-1915. It was recognized that the UBI was inadequate with regard to range, battery, armament, periscopes, and communication masts. This bought about the UBII which incorporated all the desired improvements including the addition of another periscope and communication mast, and a 5-centimeter gun. Similarly, the UCII was upgraded to improve its capabilities. These upgrades resulted in the loss of rail portability but did produce much more capable U-Boats.[28] As early as January 1916, the German Naval Staff recognized the need for more U-Boats to carry out a continued blockade, Guerre de Course, of Great Britain. The staff sent a memorandum to the Kaiser laying out the overall naval plan including the reduction of Great Britain's economy as a means to end the war. Specifically, the memo called for a significant increase in the number of available U-Boats, calling for a U-Boat fleet of 209 "ocean-going U-boats" and 60 "small U-boats" just to carry out western operations in vicinity of Great Britain and the North Sea. The numbers increased significantly when

---

[28] Rossler, 50.

adding in desired U-Boat operations in the Baltic and Mediterranean to 270 "ocean-going U-boats," 96 "small U-boats," 74 "ocean going mine-laying U-boats" and 43 "small mine-laying U-boats." The shift in thinking clearly indicates a focus on larger U-Boats at a time when Great Britain and the United States were looking towards smaller submarines based on the emergence of the smaller UB, UBII, UC and UCII-classes. The memorandum also discusses the possibility of using the larger extended range U-Boats to carry out attacks off the coast of the United States.[29]

The German Navy began work on the new larger U-Boats in 1917 with the introduction of large mine-laying submarines and the U-cruisers and continued with plans to replace the Ms U-Boats with large Ms U-Boats. However, this did not signal the end of the smaller U-Boats with an order for 24 of the new UBIII-class to be produced in 1917 as well.[30]

Despite the technological advantage held by German submarines over their British and American counterparts the U-Boat campaign was doomed to failure. With the advent of the convoy system the U-Boats were subject to attack and destruction by convoy escorts. The result was that despite the ability to roughly keep up initially with material losses, the reduction in trained submariners proved to be devastating to the U-Boat efforts in the long term. Commander Rowcliff attributed this lack of experience and training for the significant increase in U-Boats losses. 23 U-Boats were validated sunk from the beginning of 1918 through 15 April and with 9 already sunk in the first two

---

[29] Rossler, 63-65.

[30] Ibid., 66.

19

weeks of April the loss rate was rapidly increasing.[31] Germany simply could not keep up the high level of training for the remaining crews and many crews were taken from the surface fleet that was sitting stagnant in port. The overall reduction in experience led to rising losses of both U-Boats and crews and the ultimate failure of the Guerre de Course effort.

---

[31] PHGB, 1918, 691.

CHAPTER 3

U.S. SUBMARINE EMPLOYMENT

The way submarines were employed by both sides during World War I could not have been anticipated prior to the commencement of hostilities. This chapter will explore the way submarines had been thought of prior to the war and the evolution of U.S. and British tactical employment during the war for the employment of submarines and the means to counter the German U-Boat threat.

Prior to World War I, the United States had employed submarines exclusively as a defensive weapon. Officers considered submarines best for coastal and harbor defense and they were kept close to their homeport.[32] One noted naval historians wrote, "Faced with the prospect of some Japanese attempt to seize the Philippines, the United States very early deployed its own submarines to the Far East, on just this theory."[33] Secretary of the Navy, Josephus Daniels, even made an entry in his diary after meeting with Admiral Benson, the newly created Chief of Naval Operations (CNO), about "How to fortify Guam?" and that "Submarines may be better."[34] The tendency to keep the submarines close to port was due to several considerations. First, the technological development of submarine propulsion at the time precluded operations at significant distances from homeports and "submarines were just too slow to catch fast ships, even

---

[32] Weir, 5.

[33] Norman Friedman, *Submarine Design and Development* (London, UK: Conway Maritime Press, 1984), 28.

[34] Daniels, 29 June 1915, 101.

when they were surfaced."[35] The historical usage had been for attacking enemy craft only when they threatened U.S. ports. These considerations combined to relegate the submarine to a defensive role early in the war. Despite being employed in a defensive role, the utility of submarines was beginning to be understood. The Aid for Operations, Admiral Bradley A. Fiske, wrote a report to Secretary of the Navy, Josephus Daniels dated 13 May 1913. Fiske described that if the fleet were required to blockade Japan he thought the submarine in conjunction with mines and torpedoes constituted the greatest threat to the Navy.[36] Fisk continued to recognize the threat posed by the submarine and attributed the sinking of the *Bulwark*, a British battleship, on 14 November 1914 to the work of a submarine.[37] Fiske's diary entries in early February 1915 indicate that he was beginning to be aware of the increasing threat of the U-Boat, not just to the Royal Navy but also to merchant shipping.[38] Despite Fiske's notable insight, few shared his assessment of the threat.

On the eve of war in 1913, it was inconceivable to U.S. naval officers that they would confront an enemy of such a vastly different nature than what had been prepared for. The thought of using a submarine to establish control of the sea was unthinkable. Using the U.S. Navy to transport troops and protect convoys instead of fighting the

---

[35] Friedman, 36.

[36] Bradley A. Fiske, Letter dated 13 May 1913, in Joseph Daniels, *The Cabinet Diaries of Josephus Daniels, 1913-1921*, ed. David Cronon (Lincoln: University of Nebraska Press, 1963), 57.

[37] Bradley A. Fiske, *From Midshipman to Rear-Admiral* (New York: The Century Co., 1919), 562.

[38] Ibid., 573.

German fleet had not even been considered as the primary employment of the Navy.[39] In a letter to Admiral Luce from Captain Beehler, Beehler noted that the German Navy and the Emperor in particular, had been impressed with the work of Mahan and believed that "Our (Germany's) future is on the Sea."[40] With all indications that Germany was building her Navy along similar lines to the United States, any future war with Germany was expected be a decisive fleet action. The war at sea that was to come took many by surprise.

In 1915, the U.S. Navy still "discounted, by doctrine and experience, the importance of building, or even emphasizing, submarines."[41] To be fair, the Navy at the time did not believe it would be involved in the current war, rather it was concerned with a future war with Germany if they came out the victor. Wilson's neutrality policy had made the Navy focus on defending the mainland and the full offensive capability of the submarine had not been realized. There was a push by the administration to increase the number of submarines in the U.S. fleet yet the focus remained on defensive use. In 1916 as the United States began to look towards preparedness, the Naval Act of 1916 resulted in "67 submarines (9 for the fleet and 58 for the coast)."[42] The remainder of the Naval Act focused on capital ships following traditional Mahanian ideas of sea control. Jutland appeared to reinforce the belief that battleships and decisive naval action remained the

---

[39] George W. Baer, *One Hundred Years of Sea Power The U.S. Navy, 1890-1990* (Stanford, CA: Stanford University Press, 1994), 53.

[40] Albert Gleaves, *Life and Letters of Rear Admiral Stephen B. Luce, Founder of the Naval War College* (New York: The Knickerbocker Press, 1925), 302.

[41] Baer, 61.

[42] Ibid., 60.

focus of naval warfare.[43] There was still a preponderant view that the submarine was best used as a coastal defense tool. The United States at the time still did not have an appreciation for the effects of the unrestricted warfare on Great Britain. Great Britain had not been forthcoming with the United States about the U-Boat threat and just how effective they were being in attacking British shipping. Therefore, as 1917 approached, the United States was still firmly attached to its reliance on capital ships and "the doctrine of offensive sea control by capital ships reigned."[44]

With America entering the war, the submarine situation off the British coast began to be understood by the United States. The Admiralty had been less than honest with the United States about the severity of the problem and the Navy was taken by surprise on receiving word from Admiral Sims in London regarding the severity of the threat facing Britain. As of October 1917, the Germans were inflicting a loss of 500,000 tons each month making the submarine the gravest threat to the Allies.[45] The supply ships the Germans had been destroying were taking an enormous toll on the war effort.[46] "Britain herself had become dangerously vulnerable to economic warfare. Whereas during the Napoleonic Wars she had been largely self-sufficient in food, by 1924 she imported four-fifths of her wheat, two-thirds of her bacon and all of her sugar from

---

[43] Baer, 60.

[44] Ibid., 54.

[45] PHGB, 1917, 420.

[46] Baer, 67.

abroad."[47] The reliance on the import of food combined with Germany's resumption of unrestricted attacks on shipping led Great Britain to the brink of starvation by 1917. It was estimated by October 1917 that Great Britain only had five months of flour and France only had one and a half months.[48] The Guerre de Course, being indiscriminate also impacted fuel. Secretary of the Navy, Josephus Daniels noted in his diary that "Lord Northcliffe called & had a special telegram from Lloyd George: 'Must have 200,000 tons of oil Situation most serious and lack of tonnage required to bring oil fuel here from US threatens to lead to the immobilization of the Fleet'."[49] German submarines posed a grave threat to Great Britain's ability to remain in the war. A means to counter the German submarine threat had to be found to keep Britain in the war. Commander W. S. Pye described for the Board in October how the convoy system was employed to minimize the chances of German submarines finding an unprotected isolated merchant and reduce the sinking of commercial shipping.[50] By concentrating the merchants together with anti-submarine warfare (ASW) escorts, the United States and Britain significantly reduced the amount of shipping lost. Convoy operations were understood to be necessary with the knowledge that they would not be decisive for victory but could keep the war effort alive.[51] The early implementation of the convoy system involved the protection of loaded

---

[47] Brian Bond, *Britain's Two World Wars Against Germany: Myth, Memory and the Distortions of Hindsight* (Cambridge, UK: Cambridge University Press, 2014), 90.

[48] Daniels, 11 October 1917, 219.

[49] Ibid., 2 July 1917, 171.

[50] PHGB, 1917, 418.

[51] Ibid., 421.

ships inbound to Great Britain. Commander A. W. Taussig mentioned that he had been told by Captain Long that the majority, 75 percent of vessels sunk, were sunk while loaded but that shortly after implementing the convoy of inbound vessels the U-Boats shifted to attacking the empty vessels outbound from Great Britain. Taussig told the Board, "It then became necessary to adopt the convoy system for out bound vessels also."[52]

Figure 2. Electricians Mate Job Melvin Yocum on the Bridge of the L-3

Source: From author's personal collection.

---

[52] PHGB, 1917, 687.

During the war, the United States began to utilize submarines at more remote locations, stationing several classes out of Ireland, and in a more offensive manner. Boats of the K, L, O, and E-class were used for these early attempts at offensive ASW operations off the coast of Ireland and in the Azores.[53] Specifications for these classes are included in table 3.

Table 3. Specifications for E, K, L, and O-class Submarines

	E-Class	K-Class	L-Class	O-Class
Displacement	287	392 surf 521 subm	450 surf 548 subm	520.6 surf 629 subm
Length	135'3"	153'7"	167'5"	172'4"
Beam	14'7"	16'8"	17'5"	18'
Draft	11'7"	13'1"	13'7"	14'5"
Speed	14kts	14kts surf 10.5kts subm	14kts surf 10.5kts subm	14kts surf 10.5kts subm
Complement	20	28	28	29
Armament TT: Torpedo Tube 3": 3 in Deck Gun	4-18" TT	4-18" TT	1-3" 4-18" TT	1-3" 4-18" TT

Source: Created by author using data from Naval History and Heritage Command, "Dictionary of American Naval Fighting Ships—Index," US Navy, accessed 10 April 2017, https://www.history.navy.mil/research/histories/ship-histories/danfs.html.

---

[53] Carroll S. Alden, "American Submarine Operations in the War," *Proceedings* 46, no. 6 (June 1920): 811-850 and *Proceedings* 46, no. 7 (July 1920): 1013-1048, in Gary E. Weir, *Building American Submarines 1914-1940* (Washington, DC: Naval Historical Center Department of the Navy, 1991), 11.

Submarines were predominately used to protect the western approaches to the British Isles. This approach began to show the limitations of U.S. design since current U.S. submarines were not capable of maintaining open ocean operations for sufficient time to employ offensive tactics.[54] Despite submarines' inability to routinely operate at extended distances from their support bases they eventually became the greatest weapon against the U-Boat.[55] Pierce, having just returned from England where he had gone on a patrol with the British E-34 patrolling Heligoland Bight and the North Sea, commented to the Board on 9 October 1917 that, "During the last few months the British have come to the decision that submarines are one of the most important method for fighting German submarines."[56] Pierce went on to describe how the submarines operated in designated sectors and if they located a German submarine they submerged and then approached to within torpedo range to carry out an attack. Pierce gave the Board the cases of British submarines sinking German U-Boats which, as of 1 August 1917, had amounted to eleven all executed with a torpedo attack. Winterhalter felt that the submarine contributions to the ASW effort was not very significant. Pierce explained how the number of U-Boats sunk by submarines was rapidly increasing as there had been three each in 1915 and 1916 and already five in the first half of 1917 and that they were now averaging one sinking a month since the start of the submarine patrols. The sinking of

---

[54] Weir, 11.

[55] Baer, 77.

[56] PHGB, 1917, 343-344.

two in the month prior to Pierce returning home amounted to half of the total for the month.[57]

At home a more conventional approach was used. "Submarines of the N and O-classes, as well as some of the E boats, patrolled American coasts and harbors following a defensive strategy."[58] The specifications for the E, N and O-classes is included in table 4. It was found during the war that there were other uses for which submarines were better suited than surface ships. A submarine could provide covert scouting. In areas where a surface ship was unable to operate without being attacked a submarine could avoid detection and gather valuable information.[59]

Table 4. Specifications for E, N, and O-class Submarines

	E-Class	N-Class	O-Class
Displacement	287	348 surf	520.6 surf
		414 subm	629 subm
Length	135'3"	147'3"	172'4"
Beam	14'7"	15'9"	18'
Draft	11'7"	12'6"	14'5"
Speed	14kts	13kts surf	14kts surf
		11kts subm	10.5kts subm
Complement	20	25	29
Armament	4-18" TT	4-18" TT	1-3"
			4-18" TT

TT: Torpedo Tube
3": 3 in Deck Gun

Source: Created by author using data from Naval History and Heritage Command, "Dictionary of American Naval Fighting Ships—Index," US Navy, accessed 10 April 2017, https://www.history.navy.mil/research/histories/ship-histories/danfs.html.

---

[57] PHGB, 1917, 363-364.

[58] Weir, 9.

[59] Friedman, 36.

Several tactical considerations came to the fore during the war that changed the way submariners operated their ships. First was a recognition that stealth was the only true means of defense available to the submarine and that extended diving times unacceptably risked forfeiting this advantage. "During World War I it became common practice to operate with the Kingstons open, so that the main tanks were partly full, and flooded completely as soon as the vents above were opened."[60] Kingstons were the valves on the bottom of the submarine that kept water from entering the main ballast tanks. In order to flood the main ballast tanks both the kingstons and the upper vents had to be open. By operating on the surface with the vents shut and the kingstons open the main ballast tanks became partly filled with water thereby reducing the time to complete flooding and speeding the diving process. Second was the need to be able to maneuver for a prolonged period of time submerged in order to evade enemy ASW forces. In order to facilitate the ability to evade submerged for an extended amount of time it became a necessary to maintain the batteries at a high state of charge. "Wartime memoirs show almost an obsession with preserving the charge in the batteries, which was the only guarantee of a submarine's underwater mobility."[61] Another consideration that Badger asked Pierce about was the employment of a "fan arrangement" to fire multiple torpedoes at intervals to increase the likelihood of achieving a hit. Pierce explained that he felt it would help and with multiple bow tubes it was possible but that it required a lot of effort to "set each tube differently."[62]

---

[60] Friedman, 119.

[61] Ibid.

[62] PHGB, 1917, 366.

30

The largest advances in tactics and naval warfare technology were centered around countering the German submarine force. It was recognized that the Germans had a relative superiority in their submarine design, in particular it was noted that their optics were significantly ahead of both the British and U.S. designs. This relative advantage was articulated by Pye when he said that the Germans "undoubtedly sink more British boats than are lost by themselves."[63] The result was that multiple means had to be incorporated to counter the U-Boat threat. The convoy system, while arguably the most effective means of countering the threat, was only one piece of the overall strategy the Board developed. Most of the means to counter the threat were centered around the desire to commence an offensive campaign against the U-Boats. The president had expressed to Secretary Daniels his desire to start an offensive against the submarines and his frustration that the British had not also adopted the convoy system.[64] Based on the president's desires, the Board was extremely interested in getting some sort of an offensive started using any available means. The use of sea-planes, destroyers, submarine chasers, and even submarines were all discussed. The Board experienced a significant amount of frustration at the U.S. Navy's inability to rapidly commence offensive operations against the U-Boat threat. The Board felt the British were being extremely hesitant to commence any sort of offensive operations and as the Americans began to take a more active part in the war at sea it became clear that much of the current anti-submarine technology required either additional infrastructure to support operations or changes to ships' systems and tactics to be effective.

---

[63] PHGB, 1917, 419.

[64] Daniels, 3 July 1917, 172.

There was a growing desire to use aircraft for locating and cueing in surface vessels to execute an attack or to carry out a limited attack of their own. CDR E. J. King, future fleet admiral and CNO during World War II, currently serving on the staff of the Commander-in-Chief Atlantic Fleet, explained how the air platforms had been used to form what he referred to as "hunting-groups" which were being used to locate U-Boats. Several of the new air platforms could make better use of the new listening technology than surface ships by employing it from kite balloons to remove the background noise associated with employment from a surface ship.[65] Lieutenant Commander F.R.E. Davis of the Royal Naval Air Service described combined air and destroyer operations to counter the submarine. After an aircraft or blimp had sighted a submarine it called in a destroyer and continued to follow the submarine until the destroyer arrived to carry out an attack.[66] Davis also described how British aircraft had been working with submarine patrols to locate submarines and that the aircraft themselves were carrying out attacks against the U-Boats with 100-pound bombs.[67] However, in the case of the sea-planes, the lack of facilities and the shortage of planes and pilots precluded the rapid commencement of an aerial offensive.

Similarly, destroyer's maneuvering characteristics were found wanting, precluding them from being truly effective against submarines in close combat. Due to the shortcomings of destroyers, the Board spent many hearings discussing the expansion of the submarine chaser program and the rapid development of the listening technology

---

[65] PHGB, 1917, 457.

[66] Ibid., 678, 684-685.

[67] Ibid., 684.

as a means to carry out the desired offensive campaign against the submarine. Commander Submarine Force, Captain S. S. Robison, described his recommendation to start a new chaser program to build 250 new chasers and how the submarine force felt that with 250 they could make a good impact on the problem.[68] Timing of the offensive was another concern and Pye explained to the Board during his testimony on 16 October 1917 that the timing was not right for an offensive in the fall or winter and that the spring to summer of 1918 would be more conducive to commencing offensive operations. It was his recommendation that the efforts be focused on the "defense of commerce" and "the preparation for offensive operations" the following year.[69] King described what he had observed while overseas was primarily defensive in nature. King detailed how there were "in the vicinity of two thousand vessels engaged in patrol and escort work. All on account of submarines."[70]

In addition to the desired offensive campaign to counter the U-Boats, the British had been looking at mines as another possible way to address the problem. Pierce, having just returned from England discussed how the Admiralty felt that mining could "stop the submarines" if they were able to procure enough mines.[71] Additionally, King explained how the Admiralty had "filled up the Heligoland Bight with mines" in the past few months. Despite the mining in Heligoland Bight, the only effect the British believed they

---

[68] PHGB, 1917, 599.

[69] Ibid., 420.

[70] Ibid., 456.

[71] Ibid., 356.

had was to force the Germans to exit by going through "neutral territorial waters."[72] During further discussion with the Board on 19 October 1917, Pye explained that during the winter months even the mine barrage was ineffective against the U-Boats because of the inability to patrol it sufficiently due to the weather.[73] This made even a mine offensive during the winter difficult at best. Captain F. H. Schofield, later to become a member of the Board and ultimately Commander-in-Chief Battle Force, told the Board that in his opinion the mining efforts were best used to close the Straits of Dover. Schofield felt that closing the Straights of Dover would result in a significant reduction in the sinking of merchant shipping. Schofield further explained a means of using mines to attack a submarine after being found in an offensive manner. He felt that a limited minefield had a better chance of destroying a submarine than a depth charge since the depth charge had to explode in close proximity to the submarine.[74]

King explained how the British records showed that submarines were responsible for destroying more U-Boats than any other type of ASW. This was most likely due to the fact that the British were diverting most of their destroyers for convoy work and only those not engaged in convoy were assisting the submarines in countering the U-Boats.[75] Based on the success of British submarines in the anti-submarine effort against the U-

---

[72] PHGB 1917, 456.

[73] Ibid., 485.

[74] Ibid., 510.

[75] Ibid., 456.

Boats, Land submitted an estimate of the situation detailing the reasons "To place all effective American submarines in the war zone at the earliest possible date."[76]

As the war progressed, the United States became proficient in submarine operations, given the limitations of submarines at the time. Initial forays into offensive operations, while initially limited, paved the way for interwar submarine design and tactical development resulting in extremely successful submarine operations during World War II. As the technology continued to progress, the tactics evolved to take advantage of the new technology to improve submarine operations as well as the methods used to counter them. One of the most significant discoveries of the war was the use of a convoy system to protect shipping against submarine operations.

Many changes occurred during the war regarding the way a submarine should fit into a nation's naval strategy. The rising influence of the submarine could no longer be ignored and the future development and importance of the submarine to naval campaigns was just beginning to be understood. Ultimately, it was the changes in tactics facilitated by technological development that led to a continuing refinement of submarine employment and tactics. Chapter 4 will discuss the specifics of technological development and the resulting changes to submarine design and construction in the United States during the War.

In the end, the submarine played a part in the anti-submarine campaign; however the technology employed by the Allies during the war prevented them from having as dramatic an impact as they did during World War II. The German use of the submarine did solidify the importance and the utility of the submarine in the psyche of the U.S.

---

[76] PHGB, 1917, 654.

Navy. Significant efforts were subsequently implemented to improve the U.S. design and tactics to take advantage of the new technology based on lessons learned from the war and reverse engineering of captured U-Boats.[77] The next chapter will look at the specific design considerations that evolved during the war and their influence on the design of both the S-class and T-class submarines.

---

[77] Weir, 31-34.

CHAPTER 4

EVOLUTION OF SUBMARINE DESIGN, 1916-1918

During the early stages of World War I, the Board's discussions regarding submarine design centered on matching characteristics identified from German U-Boats. The Board hearings were conducted in a question and answer format where Board members asked questions of military and civilian experts to gather information about various topics. Hearings were held on topics from the use of technology and tactics the United States and Great Britain were employing at the time to changes being implemented by both Allied nations and Germany. The Board used these hearings to shape naval policy and develop design characteristics for future classes of ships. The Board of World War I was composed of the most senior officers in the Navy and as such had tremendous influence in the policy and fleet design of the Navy. The newly established CNO did not have the power to implement change in the way the Board could. The Board's discussions about submarines were largely concerned with the indications that Germany was working towards building much larger and more capable fleet submarines. The Board was also extremely interested in the development of British submarine designs since they had been engaged in ASW against Germany for more than two years.

To allow for ease of discussion, this chapter will look at submarine characteristics individually to identify what the Board was considering early in the war compared to final specifications enacted later in the war. By topic this chapter will evaluate the following characteristics: size, type of propulsion, endurance regarding size and type of motor and battery, speed, maximum submergence depth, hull characteristics regarding survivability and serviceability, primary armament, secondary armament, sensor systems to include periscopes and detection systems, signal systems, navigation equipment, and habitability systems. From this analysis this chapter will also describe the final specifications established by the Board.

Size Considerations

Commander D. F. Boyd, having just returned from Europe, spoke with the Board on 8 September 1917 regarding his experiences with British and French submarine forces. Boyd had commanded a *Bushnell* submarine tender prior to the war and therefore was a highly trusted officer due to the high profile status required for selection as commanding officer of the newest submarine tender.[78] Boyd discussed the classes of submarines the British and French were currently using and his recommendations for the updated design of U.S. submarines. Much of his discussion was centered around the size of boats being employed by the British and what their plans were for submarines best suited to the antisubmarine effort. Boyd discussed how the British were moving away from larger fleet submarines towards smaller 400-ton submarines. His advice to the Board was "If the situation is such that a large number of submarines is needed and reliability was sought and that the Department was unwilling to try out any new device I should say a large number of small submarines of about the H-type of the British and our own would be advisable."[79] During this hearing, Winterhalter made a statement indicating a general lack of understanding regarding the current state of U.S. submarine

---

[78] Don McGrogan, "USS Bushnell," NavSource Naval History, accessed 15 February 2017, http://www.navsource.org/archives/09/36/3602.htm.

[79] PHGB, 1917, 178.

design when he said, "We should be able to duplicate here anything abroad in submarines."[80] While at the time, the United States had a detailed understanding of British and French submarine design, little information was available to the Americans regarding German submarines.

Boyd's recommendation for the smaller submarine came with another recommendation, that they should be used for coastal defense or submarine patrol. Where he began to depart from the common wisdom at the time was that he thought that they could also be employed for "distant service it having been proved by experience that they are able to keep the seas."[81] The British were building an H-Class boat similar to the US L-Class and the Germans were building a 350-ton mine-layer.[82] Boyd also brought to the Board's attention the ability of the submarine to conduct ASW. One naval officer, LT Varley, had recommended pursuing the smaller submarine design and continuing with the H-class but he was ultimately discredited due to the discovery that he had been influenced by Electric Boat to recommend the smaller boats.[83] The contractor viewed the smaller submarines as more cost effective and they would not have to spend additional capital on research and development.

One of the driving factors for the Board considering a larger submarine had to do with habitability. The shift to an 800-ton boat was being considered in order to improve

---

[80] PHGB, 1917, 178.

[81] Ibid., 179.

[82] Ibid., 188.

[83] Ibid., 1918, 541.

habitability.[84] A larger submarine allowed for more room for atmospheric control equipment to ensure the air quality was sufficient to allow the crew to keep the submarine at sea for longer periods of time. A compromise had to be reached that could afford the smallest size possible while meeting the desire for improved habitability.

In looking at size, the comparison was drawn to the existing L, O, and R-class submarines. The L-class with a submerged displacement of 527 tons, and the O and R-classes being 50 and 100 tons heavier respectively.[85] The general trend had been towards a larger boat that improved habitability and allowed for ease of access to make final adjustments on torpedoes prior to time of fire. The adjustment was necessary to improve accuracy and likelihood of a successful hit.

Propulsion Systems

At the onset of war, the U.S. Congress wanted the Navy to build a 25-knot submarine. The only way a submarine could reach 25 knots was by using a steam propulsion system since diesel engines were not capable of generating the required horsepower. The British had built a steam submarine, the K-class that was purported to achieve 25 knots however the design had some serious drawbacks. In using a steam propulsion system, the residual heat had to be accounted for and such a system required a means to dispose of the excess heat after submerging or a lengthy cool down time was required prior to submerging. After looking at the possibility of a U.S. steam submarine and identifying how the British were employing the K-class it was determined that a

---

[84] PHGB, 1917, 371.

[85] Ibid., 377.

steam model was incompatible with the design considerations for U.S. submarines. A true steam submarine did not come into existence until the age of nuclear power in the 1950s.

The M-1 employed a cross-head type two-cycle diesel engine that Pierce thought were the best available. Pierce had just returned from England where he had gone on patrol with the E-34 in Heligoland Bight and the North Sea. The engine being considered for the new design was a New London Ship and Engine Company (Nelesco) 4-cycle diesel. Nelesco was a subsidiary of Electric Boat, one of the two primary contractors for building U.S. submarines and had been building diesels for Electric Boat since the F-class.[86] Despite setbacks caused by storage battery problems, Pierce informed the Board on 9 October 1917 that the M-1 would be ready by "The 15th of next month."[87]

A link between the engines and detection ranges with the newly developed listening devices like the C tube and the Mason apparatus was identified during the hearing on 13 November 1917. Captain R. H. Leigh, discussed how the G-1 could effectively avoid detection by running its engines at a lower revolution than the other submarines. Even though the G-1 was only able to maintain this reduced engine speed for eight minutes it did allow her to avoid detection during the reduced speed run.[88] The difficulty with maintaining such a slow speed as Leigh described is that the lack of speed makes depth control more difficult. As Leigh put it when Badger asked about the speed

---

[86] Weir, 9, 119.

[87] PHGB, 1917, 359.

[88] Ibid., 532.

34 revolutions would get for the G-1 "So slow she would have to come to the top or go to the bottom after eight minutes."[89]

Endurance

During the hearing on 6 September 1917, Winterhalter mentioned, "According to the German accounts they are building what they call cruisers of 2,400 tons with two motors of 150 millimeters and these are building at the Krupp works and two were launched last February."[90] These new U-cruisers were expected to have significant improvements in endurance over the previous U-Boats. The focus of this hearing was to establish the new submerged endurance requirement for U.S. submarines. Badger wanted to set the requirements at nine knots for two hours and five knots for 20 hours during the hearing on 6 September 1917.[91] The desire was to achieve a submerged endurance of 100 nautical miles on a single charge resulting in the five knot for 20-hour requirement. The 100 nautical miles gave a submarine the ability to spend sufficient time submerged to avoid detection and if necessary open range from a counterattack. It had been identified by LCDR J. O. Fisher that the battery proposed was insufficient to support the combined requirements and that "Five knots for 20 hours would require four times as large a battery. That is, roughly. With nine knots maximum we can get about five knots for four hours."[92] Fisher identified for the Board how the combination of the battery and the

---

[89] PHGB, 1917, 587.

[90] Ibid., 134.

[91] Ibid., 111.

[92] Ibid., 135.

motor determined a submarine's endurance. The motor had to be sized according to the maximum speed desired which when put in combination with a given battery capacity at a given discharge rate determined the number of hours a submarine could travel at a given speed. An additional consideration regarding the size of the motor was its impact on charging time of the batteries when on the surface. "You have a motor for 9 knots and a battery for 5 knots for 20 hours. It will only deliver current at a certain rate. The current that motor will give as a generator will not be sufficient to charge that battery in the minimum time. You might have to take 10 or 12 hours. That is a decided disadvantage."[93] Having to spend 10 to 12 hours recharging the batteries meant that a submarine was forced to spend an inordinate amount of time in a vulnerable condition because a submarine charging its batteries on the surface is much more vulnerable to detection and subsequent prosecution. In the event a submarine was forced to submerge prior to having fully charged the battery the submerged endurance was reduced accordingly with the available charge on the battery. Winterhalter properly identified that "If we concede all you say and take the enormous increase of battery we will be building the submarine for the battery. We have got to sacrifice. We are forced to this conclusion that we could not provide a battery big enough without building a submarine for the battery."[94] In further discussions attempting to reduce the size of the battery it was considered to lower the minimum speed to 1.5 knots to achieve a higher endurance. Badger identified the problem with this when he said "From all I have heard three knots is the lowest speed which we can consider reasonably for controlling the boat. 1-1/2 is

---

[93] PHGB, 1917, 132.

[94] Ibid., 139.

not enough."[95] This is a simple matter of speed being required to provide enough lifting force to allow a submarine to overcome negative buoyancy produced from an improper trim. If a boat is too heavy, then speed is required for the submarine moving through the water at an up angle in combination with the bow planes and stern planes to produce sufficient lift to compensate for the weight to keep the boat at a given depth. During hearings on 11 October 1917 with Land and 21 December 1917 with Mr. Goodall the endurance requirements were ultimately set to 20 hours at five knots and maximum speed for one hour.[96]

It must also be recognized that diesel fuel storage and engine performance are only one component of endurance. The second component of endurance is human endurance. Sufficient stores must be brought onboard to feed and care for the crew. On 11 October 1917, the discussion question of provisions and stores arose. The original specification of 30 days came into question. It was not felt that 30 days was achievable on a smaller boat, Winterhalter and Land both felt that 30 days was too long for the type of assignments expected for the new class. Land told the Board "There is no use trying to bluff ourselves. They don't get it."[97] Robison met with the Board on 15 November 1917 and described how the K-boats were only able to stay at sea for 12 days due to food and water storage. The inability to carry sufficient supplies added credence for building the slightly larger 800-ton boats as a means to increase the human endurance.

---

[95] PHGB, 1917, 140.

[96] Ibid., 381, 751.

[97] Ibid., 384.

Speed and Depth Considerations

Winterhalter identified on 5 September 1917 during a hearing with Naval Constructor Stocker that U.S. Congress had set a speed requirement of 25 knots. Stocker informed the Board that 25 knots was unachievable with a diesel engine.[98] The only way to achieve speeds that high was to use steam turbine propulsion. The downside of a steam propulsion system being residual heat delaying submarine diving time to allow for cooling down the boiler. Additionally, a steam propulsion system could do nothing to improve submerged speed performance of a submarine which is only dependent on the size of the motor and the battery. During Boyd's meeting with the Board on 8 September 1917, the Board was interested in the speed specification of British submarines and what Boyd thought was best for the U.S. designs. Boyd, consistent with previous testimony by Chief of the Bureau of Construction and Repair, Admiral D. W. Taylor, on 6 September 1917, thought a maximum submerged speed of nine knots would suffice.[99] Discussion arose on 11 October 1917 regarding a higher submerged speed of 15 knots in order to allow a submarine to press an attack submerged. Land felt that 15 knots might be possible with only one propeller and modifications to the lines but that the idea should be referred to Steam Engineering to evaluate it further, however when further pressed by Badger he identified that in a larger boat he did not believe the speed was achievable.[100] Pierce described how British submariners were increasing their submerged depth at periscope depth to achieve higher speeds. The ability of a submarine to operate at higher speed at a

---

[98] PHGB, 1917, 102.

[99] Ibid., 106, 187.

[100] Ibid., 379.

deeper submergence depth, especially at periscope depth, is because as a submarine proceeds deeper it is less affected by wave action and has an increased pressure on the propeller due to the deeper depth. For a given depth in water, the weight of the water above it increases the pressure felt on all exterior surfaces of a submarine. The combined effect being that as the submarine is then capable of a higher speed than at the shallower depth. Pierce explained how British submarines were shifting to a 30-foot periscope instead of a 25-foot periscope to take advantage of this concept. In conjunction with the longer periscope, British submarines were also shifting to a larger periscope shear in order to support the periscope.[101] The shear was a means of supporting the barrel of the periscope to prevent the barrel from being damaged by higher submerged speeds. This is the precursor to the modern fairing used to support a periscope barrel. The final determination from all the discussions on 11 October 1917 came down to a submerged speed of nine knots for a fleet submarine and a motor able to take the current at a one-hour discharge rate.[102]

During Robison's discussions with the Board on 15 November 1917, Winterhalter identified that the British were considering 15 knots submerged speed for an offensive submarine. Robison pointed out that while 15 knots submerged is achievable over a short period it is not sustainable for longer ones. This again points to the relationship between speed and battery capacity. The submergence depth was considered during a hearing with Taylor on 9 September 1917 and based on the welding and framing technology for submarines at the time was limited to 150-feet test depth with a factor of safety of 200

---

[101] PHGB, 1917, 379.

[102] Ibid., 384.

feet.[103] The depth specification was confirmed during the hearing with Land on 11 October 1917.[104] The only means available to test the watertight integrity of a submarine at the time prior to sea trials was to conduct a hydrostatic test pier-side. Winterhalter and Taylor discussed including a 60-pound hydrostatic test as sufficient for this purpose.[105]

Hull Characteristics

Board discussions of the framing, welding, and lines were predominant concerns initially. The decision as to a single hull or a double hull and the evaluation of what the British and Germans were building, was discussed by the Board. The R-class was built using a single hull design and had been built for both the British and the U.S. Navy.[106] The final decision implemented in the U.S. Navy S-class was a double hull design while the EB built T-class was to use a single hull.[107] Other concerns that arose due to the German use of Zeppelins caused the Board to discuss possible means of painting the hulls in order to reduce the ability of Zeppelins and seaplanes from recognizing a submerged submarine.[108] During the 11 October hearing, Winterhalter also discussed the compartment specification. "Retain positive buoyancy in a light condition with any compartment flooded."[109] This method of compartmentation meant heavier internal

---

[103] PHGB, 1917, 106,109.

[104] Ibid., 369.

[105] Ibid., 109.

[106] Ibid., 750.

[107] Ibid., 1918, 371.

[108] Ibid., 843.

[109] Ibid., 1917, 369.

bulkheads but assisted a submarine to avoid being lost due to a flooding casualty in any individual compartment.

Primary Armament

Regarding torpedo tubes and weapons storage, the Board considered the location and number of torpedo tubes to be built into the next design. CDR Kearny had noted that the British were using broadside tubes.[110] A broadside tube was a tube that was mounted amidships either internal to the hull or external and mounted on the deck. Winterhalter identified that for the number of torpedoes to be carried the Board was currently planning on "An allowance of 12 torpedoes for the bow and four for the broadside."[111] The discussion regarding the number of torpedoes to be carried identified that in the event broadside tubes were eliminated additional storage for weapons or for more frequent reloading from a tender would be required. CDR D. C. Bingham, just back from inspecting British naval development, identified that by 16 October 1917 the British had begun removing broadside tubes from their most recent designs.[112] The Board continued looking at broadside tubes and the submarine design for the AA-1, what was later reclassified as the T-1, was fitted with an experimental broadside tube.[113] The number of torpedoes that should be available came up again periodically, the consensus being that for each tube there should be a spare inboard. The British were allowing for one reload of

---

[110] PHGB, 1917, 203.

[111] Ibid., 203.

[112] Ibid., 452.

[113] Ibid., 1918, 916.

each tube for a total of 12 14-inch torpedoes. Early U.S. designs had employed an 18-inch torpedo, however these were abandoned by the time of the R-class. For the S-class and the T-class the 21-inch torpedoes were ultimately selected.[114]

As it began to be recognized that the largest impact on German submarines was coming from Allied submarines, a renewed focus on torpedo construction and employment began to emerge. King described how regarding the torpedo, the British were looking at developing a smaller high speed torpedo and modifying torpedo employment to include a means of launching a salvo to increase the likelihood of achieving a hit.[115]

Whether to carry mines in future designs was also a major point of discussion. Germany had begun building numerous mine laying submarines and it made the Board question if the United States should consider building mine laying submarines of their own. Board member Captain Marvell identified that he did not believe they were required at the time as there was not a practical way to employ them against Germany.[116] Marvell felt that there was no need to build a mine specific submarine and that they should not be employed from existing classes either. "There is not room enough and they can't carry enough mines."[117] Board member Captain Belknap also did not think the United States needed a mine laying submarine.[118] During the hearing on 11 October 1917 the Board

---

[114] PHGB, 1917, 186-187.

[115] Ibid., 456.

[116] Ibid., 235.

[117] Ibid.

[118] Ibid., 330.

tabled the discussion of mine laying submarines for the time being to focus on the fleet submarines. If a mine laying submarine became necessary both Pierce and Land felt that an existing submarine could be modified to carry mines in lieu of building a mine specific class of submarine.

Secondary Armament

The Board was interested in ensuring sufficient wet guns on future designs. The concern was that by providing additional deck guns the speed would be affected. Early discussion was based on towing basin testing and it was noted by Commander T. A. Kearney "the loss of speed was a little bigger than in actual service."[119] The Board was beginning to look at alternative mounting methods to increase the deck gun capacity and allow for two guns to include a 3-inch anti-aircraft gun.[120] However, there were some differing opinions on the number of guns. Land, along with Board members General Barnett and Captain Shoemaker, believed that there should only be one gun on a submarine but that the ammunition should be increased.[121]

Sensor Systems

Another important aspect that was just coming into being was the development of hydrophones, the predecessor of Sound Navigation and Ranging (SONAR). The Board referred to this technology as listening devices and Admiral Griffin had formed a committee, as part of the National Research Council, to focus on experimenting with the

---

[119] PHGB, 1917, 202.

[120] Ibid., 202.

[121] Ibid., 376.

new listening devices on submarines. Major R. A. Millikan, a noted U.S. Army physicist and future Nobel Prize for Physics winner in 1923, was selected as the new committees chairman.[122] This predecessor to SONAR, while rudimentary at the time, gave the Allies for the first time the ability to identify that a submarine was present even when it was submerged. The detection range of this early sensor was extremely limited, however it did allow submarine chasers the ability to listen for a submarine and to identify its general direction. After initial demonstrations on submarine chasers there were experiments with installing them on submarines. The first installment went through the deck of the submarine in an arrangement that precluded use when the submarine was surfaced. Planning was begun for a means to install the sensor through the hull of the submarine allowing for use on the surface and when submerged. The concern with a through hull installation was that the detector component would be damaged in the event the submarine was required to bottom itself. Schofield described on 12 October 1917 how the initial submarine installation on the L-10 and the N-1 were installed through the keel to allow for operation to listen on the surface.[123] Leigh identified that it was able to be housed which prevented damage.[124] Schofield discussed how Professor Mason was working on improving the performance of the C tubes but they had not made much headway yet. Schofield also discussed how the Submarine Listening school was improving the operators' ability and that when trained operators were able to identify submarines at a distance of one to two miles. It is worthwhile to note that Lieutenant

---

[122] PHGB, 1918, 83.

[123] PHGB, 1917, 393.

[124] Ibid., 307.

McCormack identified that Mr. Hewitt, a member of the Naval Consulting Board, felt that the U.S. C tube was a superior hydrophone to all British hydrophones in use.[125] As the work on listening devices progressed, the importance of placing them onboard submarines began to be identified. Taylor described how he believed that submarines were ideal to be fitted with the new listening devices.[126] When Millikan testified before the Board he explained how the Nahant group had been formed as a means to consolidate the expertise of the three major companies conducting work in the submarine detection field, the General Electric Company, the Western Electric Company, and the Submarine Signaling Company.[127] It was this Nahant group, based out of Western Electric Company in Nahant, Massachusetts, that made possible the relatively rapid advancement of the U.S. submarine detection technology compared to the British and the French.[128] Another development that Millikan brought to the Board's attention was a possible high frequency method of locating a submarine by transmitting a pulse and listening for a return. This type of active SONAR was recognized by Millikan as a short-range method due to the limited range of high frequency waves but the possibility for future development was recognized as well as other possible uses as a communication device.[129]

The continuing development of the new listening technology, toward what became SONAR, resulted in the development of a towable hydrophone, called the fish

---

[125] PHGB, 1917, 465.

[126] Ibid., 674.

[127] PHGB, 1918, 84.

[128] Weir, 73.

[129] PHGB, 1918, 99-103.

hydrophone, that allowed a ship to listen for submarines without having to shut down its own machinery. This new hydrophone allowed for a vessel to remain moving while still monitoring for an enemy submarine. "The Admiralty feel that this fish hydrophone will be a great help in eliminating the submarine menace"[130] At the time of Pierce's testimony to the Board, the United States was not in possession of this new fish hydrophone. Schofield discussed the U.S. development of what they were calling a "drifter set."[131] This U.S. version of the fish hydrophone allowed for detection at up to 12 miles. The researchers at Boston were making significant progress by combining the C tube research and the new drifter set. It was felt that they could identify a submarines direction with the drifter set within 30 degrees for an inexperienced observer and 10 degrees with training.[132] When King testified on 17 October 1917, he described the benefits of the new towable hydrophone as being able to operate "at speeds up to ten knots."[133] This allowed a surface ship to move against a submarine as opposed to being much more vulnerable and stopping to listen. A stationary ship is much more vulnerable to attack than a ship making way. Experiments carried out from New London with the submarine chaser *Narada* and the new Mason apparatus were proving to increase the range of detection significantly. The Mason apparatus had been developed by Professor Mason from the University of Wisconsin working at New London over the summer of 1917 and consisted

---

[130] PHGB, 1917, 357.

[131] Ibid., 391.

[132] Ibid., 392.

[133] Ibid., 457.

of multiple "Broca tubes on either side of the keel of the vessel."[134] Detection ranges from the *Narada* trials were out to seven to eight miles with the *Narada* operating at a speed of up to 11 knots.[135] Leigh discussed the Mason apparatus during his meeting with the Board on 13 November 1917. Leigh described how that with the wind blowing at "5 or 6" and with the submarines periscope "just awash," the Mason apparatus was able to provide a direction that the crew could use to relocate the submarine when her periscope was no longer held visually due to whitecaps.[136] Leigh felt that the test results proved that the Mason apparatus was superior to the conventional C tube for locating a submarine. Leigh went on to describe how the new K tube was being used to mount receivers 70 feet from each other and allow the listener to move the two receivers to determine a bearing within eight degrees. Millikan also described for the Board how the K tube and the Mason device allowed for further detection ranges as well as an improvement in bearing resolution over the earlier C tubes.[137] This new arrangement also let the user make an approximation of range.[138] Leigh finished his discussion by detailing how he thought a combination of C tubes, K tubes and a triangle formation of multiple submarine chasers could be used to locate and maintain contact with a submarine to allow the chasers to coordinate an attack.[139]

---

[134] PHGB, 1917, 582.

[135] Ibid.

[136] Ibid., 583.

[137] PHGB, 1918, 95-98.

[138] PHGB, 1917, 587.

[139] Ibid., 590.

Navigation and Signals Equipment

The only significant navigational advancement from the earlier classes to the S-class was the inclusion of two gyrocompasses. The gyrocompass allowed for a submarine to overcome the inherent problems of using a magnetic compass in an enclosed metal hull where the hull itself made the use of a magnetic compass problematic at best. Land noted during a hearing that the Russian H boats were not equipped with a gyroscope to conserve space but that for U.S. designs, the gyrocompass was considered essential.[140]

While at periscope depth, nothing provides as much situational awareness as the periscope. Bingham had been impressed with the British periscopes during his visit to Europe and felt them to be superior to the optics employed on surfaces ships.[141]

A significant problem existed with positively identifying a friendly submarine to friendly forces to prevent fratricide. Several British submarines had been lost to friendly fire for having been misidentified as a German submarine. During discussions on 11 October 1917, Pierce mentioned that as a possible means of mitigating this problem in the future, the British had been using lights as recognition signals. The light was projected using a periscope tube to make it visible even before the submarine surfaced and had been tried out on the G-1.[142] Pierce and Winterhalter felt that some type of recognition signal should be included in the U.S. design. Millikan described one possible signaling device that had been found during research on the listening devices. A high frequency pulse could be sent through the water in the 50,000-100,000 hertz range that

---

[140] PHGB, 1918, 483.

[141] PHGB, 1917, 454.

[142] Ibid., 382.

allowed a submarine to signal through the water in a frequency range that could not be heard by current listening devices and therefore was able to provide a secure means of signaling both to and from a submarine.[143]

Radio sets for submarines were discussed by McCormack on 17 October 1917 where he identified the current radio configuration on British submarines. McCormack mentioned that they were using a 3.5-kilowatt arc set that could achieve a range of 250-300 miles. The antennae were attached as follows: "They have two antennae, one rigged permanently from bow to stern and attached to the periscopes, and another on the side with either hinged or telescopic mast."[144] For a submarine redundancy is extremely important as a failure of an individual component does not result in an inability to carry out a mission.

Habitability Systems

The Board was also interested in the habitability of submarines. Badger thought this curious because the United States felt "the 450-ton boat is too small for habitability and have practically stopped building them."[145] Boyd discussed the need to refresh the air but that advances had been made, specifically he identified that "The ventilation troubles can be easily straightened out . . . If they stayed out three days before they thought they

---

[143] PHGB, 1918, 101-102.

[144] PHGB, 1917, 464.

[145] Ibid., 188.

were doing great things. Now they stay out a month."[146] During the testimony of Pierce, Badger inquired about the habitability of the E-class. Pierce identified:

> The air was quite bad, very bad, toward the end of the day and it was found necessary to start the air-purifiers going. The American boats are not equipped with those as they should be, and I suppose it is because the Americans have not considered it necessary to operate under water for so long a time as is now being done. The British have air-purifiers in all their boats. It consists of a motor which draws the air through chemicals.[147]

During further questioning by the Board, Pierce talked about the adverse effects on personnel caused by environmental conditions on the E-class. The resulting impact of the environmental conditions required ten days in port for submariners to recover before going out again.[148] In comparison to the British, U.S. submarines were judged by Naval Constructor W. G. DuBose to be superior to the British designs "in most cases."[149] Winterhalter identified that there was a correlation between the size of the boat and the success of the ventilation systems during discussions with Surgeon General of the Navy, W. C. Braisted, on 1 November 1917 and that the British H-class was "superior to the larger submarines except in the question of ventilation."[150] Dr. Braisted identified that the Navy had obtained a "soda-lime" device from the British and were maintaining them at New London.[151]

---

[146] PHGB, 1917, 190.

[147] Ibid., 351.

[148] Ibid., 354.

[149] Ibid., 472.

[150] Ibid., 547.

[151] Ibid.

Robison explained to the Board how the new air purifying equipment, "known as the 'Gibbs' machine" testing on the K and L-classes had maintained adequate breathing air during a 48-hour test. The "Gibbs" machine consisted of a 40-pound can of soda lime driven by a one-quarter-horsepower motor that combined weighed 65-70 pounds.[152] Robison had gone onboard immediately after the test and informed the Board that the personnel were "perfectly comfortable."[153] William E. Gibbs of the Bureau of Mines spoke with the Board on 20 November 1917 and described the development of the technology to remove carbon dioxide from the air. The idea had come from a Dr. J. S. Haldane who had developed a "new form of soda lime" that he suggested the Bureau of Mines use in their rescue device.[154] Gibbs had identified that the technology was well suited to the submarine environment based on its confined spaces. He had adapted several devices that were used in the 48-hour tests and described how the air was better following the test than at the beginning.[155] Gibbs initially wanted four units in each submarine, one for each compartment, however space considerations resulted in the number being reduced to two.[156] Gibbs informed the Board that the device required 10 cans for a 48-hour period.[157]

---

[152] PHGB, 1917, 620.

[153] Ibid., 605.

[154] Ibid., 617.

[155] Ibid., 618.

[156] Ibid., 619.

[157] Ibid., 621.

Another habitability consideration was the supply of oxygen. To stay submerged for any extended period of time required a supply of oxygen to maintain sufficient levels for personnel safety. Gibbs identified 500 feet of oxygen was required for the same 48-hour period as the carbon dioxide test.[158] Therefore, to facilitate extended submerged operations the submarines were fitted with tanks to hold compressed oxygen that could be vented into the submarine to replenish the oxygen supply. Gibbs described the tanks used as "cylinders compressed to 120 atmospheres which weigh in the neighborhood of 100 pounds each. They are about 5 feet long and 8 inches in diameter."[159] He went on to describe how for seven days a boat needed 1,400 pounds of soda lime and 1,750 feet of oxygen with a net result that a submarine could operate "free from the tender for a week and remain under 20 hours each day."[160]

Control of the hydrogen produced by battery charging and discharging, also needed addressing to allow for extended submerged operations. A hydrogen concentration of 10 percent presented an explosion hazard and even a concentration of 5 percent was a fire hazard. Gibbs discussed a possible means of disposing of the hydrogen with a small device that could filter out and burn the hydrogen in a controlled manner.[161] Assistant Surgeon E. F. DuBois, U.S. Navy Reserve Force similarly discussed wanting to limit hydrogen to no more than 3 percent to prevent a fire or explosion hazard.[162] Land

---

[158] PHGB, 1917, 621.

[159] Ibid.

[160] Ibid.

[161] Ibid., 619.

[162] Ibid., 637.

discussed with the Board on 22 November 1917 that a method for measuring hydrogen, called the Sperry apparatus, using a Wheatstone bridge was being developed for use onboard submarines. A Wheatstone bridge works using the nature of hydrogen, which produces a cooling effect which when run across a resistor changes the resistance producing a corresponding change in voltage that can be measured and a hydrogen concentration can be determined by the change in voltage. Land described this Sperry apparatus as being "complicated and expensive" but that a Burrill hydrogen detector had been issued to each boat that was easier to use and could still be performed onboard.[163] Land also felt that the Board should include a means for measuring and eliminating hydrogen in the future design.[164]

While at the time of DuBois's testimony, no method for handling carbon monoxide had been developed, he mentioned that Professor Frazer of Johns Hopkins was working on a means of dealing with it.[165] Other toxic gases, like chlorine gas, DuBois felt could be dealt with by simply donning the Navy mask, a similar mask to the Army mask developed to deal with chemical weapons introduced on the European battlefields.[166] Chlorine gas was the product of seawater interacting with an electric current, most notably occurring in the battery compartments. Other means to handle chlorine gas were implemented in the form of a change to the battery cell design which were designed to

---

[163] PHGB, 1917, 646.

[164] Ibid., 648.

[165] Ibid., 639.

[166] Ibid., 640.

prevent seawater introduction into the cells thereby eliminating the source of chlorine gas production.[167]

As a result of all the atmospheric considerations, monitoring for gasses was identified as a means to extend the life of the soda lime and the oxygen bottles. A means of measuring the carbon dioxide by use of the "Orsatt apparatus" allowed the crew to wait until carbon dioxide rose to a level that required filtering.[168] Gibbs was more concerned with oxygen as the effects of low oxygen were not as identifiable as the presence of carbon dioxide and had been developing a device to measure the oxygen concentration. The recommendation Gibbs made was to never let oxygen fall below 17 percent and to use a continuous bleed type delivery to avoid a mistake resulting in excessively low concentrations that could render the crew incapacitated.[169] Gibbs identified that a bleed rate of "20 cubic feet an hour is sufficient for a crew of 23 men."[170] While DuBois also agreed with the 17 percent limit for oxygen, he identified that as the point when oxygen would be supplied from the tanks. With the inclusion of monitoring for gas concentrations and devices to do so, the early signs of modern day submarine atmospheric control appear. The Board also questioned DuBois on 21 November 1917 about atmospheric controls. Like Gibbs, DuBois identified the need to control carbon dioxide below 3 percent as well as to devise a measuring device to determine when the

---

[167] PHGB, 1917, 649.

[168] Ibid., 623.

[169] Ibid., 624.

[170] Ibid., 628.

soda lime device had to be started.[171] DuBois also believed that a method for determining oxygen concentration should be developed for practical use onboard a submarine.[172] The recommendation of Gibbs and DuBois reflected the Bureau of Construction and Repair *Instructions for Use of Air Purifying Apparatus and Compressed Air in Submarines* dated 10 November 1917 which called for a 3 percent and 17 percent limit for carbon dioxide and oxygen respectively.[173]

<u>Consolidated Specification Summary</u>

During the Board's discussion with Boyd on 8 September 1917, Winterhalter laid out the current design considerations for what eventually become the T-Class. "In this boat here, 2400 tons or more, 5 officers and 50 men, with a battery of two 5-inch guns, one 3-inch anti-aircraft gun, 21-inch torpedoes, four bow tubes and one 21-inch tube on each broadside, with the radius prescribed and stores for 45 days"[174] Despite numerous hearings on design characteristics throughout the war, the basis for the final specifications enacted as the war came to a close had been identified as early as September of 1917.

Early in the war during a hearing on 11 October 2017, the Board discussed with Land how many of each class were being built. Land identified that there were currently

---

[171] Ibid., 636.

[172] PHGB, 1917, 639.

[173] Ibid., 646a.

[174] Ibid., 187.

62

25 that would be commissioned by June "Fourteen O-boats, 7 N-Boats and 4 L-boats."[175] Winterhalter wanted to know if there was room to start work on one of the classes the Board was currently working on. Land brought to the Board's attention that the current boats were being immediately followed by R-class and S-class boats that had already been contracted for. Land also presented the Board with a comparison of the S-class to the H-class "Showing improvements and added equipment in the S-class."[176] The detailed report is included in table 5.

---

[175] PHGB, 1917, 386.

[176] PHGB, 1918, 544-545.

Table 5. S-class Improvements over H-class

1. 50 to 75% more torpedoes.
2. Can carry a gun.
3. Can carry proper ammunition allowance (50% more than 600 ton boats.
4. Greater reliable surface speed and radius of action.
5. Greater submerged speed and radius of action.
6. Proper ventilation for main motors.
7. Proper ventilation for motor room.
8. Proper ventilation for torpedo room.
9. Housing periscopes – Proper housing lengths.
10. Alti-periscope – anti-aeroplane instruments.
11. Submarine Signal Set.
12. Wireless apparatus – mast, 2 K.W. set, etc.
13. 3 man conning tower.
14. Two Gyro Compasses.
15. Chariot Bridge.
16. Four machine tools – lathe, drill, grinder, etc.
17. Evaporator.
18. Distiller.
19. Fresh water tanks for battery water.
20. Bunk for each member of crew.
21. Lockers for each member of crew.
22. Provisions for thirty days.
23. Refrigerating Outfit.
24. Independently driven auxiliaries – air compressors – bilge pumps, oil pumps, circulating water pumps.
25. More efficient batteries – much heavier than formerly.
26. Air purifying apparatus.
27. Hydrogen detectors.
28. Hydrogen eliminators.
29. Target Bearing Indicators.
30. Sound Detecting Devices – various types.
31. Cork sheathing.
32. Marker Buoy.
33. Fireless Cooker.
34. Fire extinguishers.
35. Running lights in conning tower.
36. Torpedo work bench, tool locker and equipment.
37. Enlarged Torpedo Room.
38. Adequate torpedo loading equipment.
39. Two W. C's.
40. Proper mess gear equipment.
41. Pneumereator System.
42. Confidential Locker.
43. Anchor (deck) housed in hawse pipe.
44. Towing gear operable inside of boat.
45. Chart Board.
46. Clearing Lines and Jumping Wires – Sounding Machine.

Source: Created by author using data from *Proceedings and Hearings of the General Board of the US Navy, 1900-1950,* vol. 1-2, 14 August-31 December 1918, Archival Information Record Group 80, Combined Arms Research Library, Fort Leavenworth, KS, (microfilm), 544-545.

Early in the war, the growing consensus was that the U.S. H-Boats were better suited as general-purpose submarines than the British K-Boats. DuBose described on 17 October 1917 how "considering only operating features the 'H' boats are much handier all around than their 'K' boats."[177] There was a time when the Board sought to secure a smaller design. It was through the consistent work of submariners, in particular the efforts of Land that the Board began looking at alternatives to the smaller submarines towards a slightly larger more capable platform. Robison's largest concern was the inability of the contractors to deliver completed boats. "They show 99% completion, but remain in the hands of the contractors for months waiting while they are endeavoring to meet some specification on which they have failed."[178] Lake had shown through a series of labor problems that they needed a change in management.[179] Similarly, Land described how the progress was insufficient and by peace time standard production was only at 2/10 vice 10/10. Winterhalter agreed that progress must be improved to meet 99 boats for 1918.[180] Land described how the 99 boats being currently built for completion in 1918 met the need. Specifically, Land wrote to the Board "No new designs are necessary. No new construction need be authorized. The problem is in hand. The one thing required is governmental pressure behind two private concerns and one navy yard."[181] With the

---

[177] PHGB, 1917, 472.

[178] Ibid., 607.

[179] Ibid., 608.

[180] Ibid., 652.

[181] Ibid., 656.

approval of the S-class, the debate over building smaller submarines was finally ended and no longer would the Navy consider the smaller 300 to 400-ton submarines.

The overall design hearing effort during World War I resulted in the finalization of the S and T-class designs. The efforts undertaken by the Board during the war led to the shift in control of submarine design away from the manufacturers and transferred it to the Navy. The Navy now having control over design prior to production allowed the Navy to dictate what technological development would be pursued as opposed to the manufacturers building a submarine without sufficient input from the submariners. Ultimately the S-class and the experimental T-class became the model for interwar development of the fleet submarines that would dominate in the Pacific during World War II. The next chapter will analyze the overall impacts of the Board's involvement in submarine design during the war on submarine development and the shift in naval thinking produced by the new possibilities for submarines.

CHAPTER 5

CONCLUSIONS

Germany's introduction of unrestricted submarine warfare during World War I led to a rapid change in the thinking of Navy leaders in the United States and Great Britain, about the tactical employment of submarines, their design and construction, and the best means to counter the new submarine threat. The evolution in thinking was reflected in the Board hearings throughout the war and had dramatic impacts on the submarine force and the Navy. No longer could the United States continue its Mahanian influenced buildup of battleships as the answer for achieving naval supremacy at sea.[182] Smaller, more capable anti-submarine platforms came to dominate conventional U.S. naval construction during the war with the rise of the destroyer and the submarine chasers. These changes were vital to countering the German U-Boat threat and allowed Great Britain to remain in the war and allowed the United States to bring troops and supplies to Europe to sustain the allied war effort.

The adoption of the convoy system forced the German U-Boats to attack the Allies at their points of strength, and therefore this was where the Allied naval forces had the most success. This reminds one of the strategies proposed by the noted British theorist Sir Julian Corbett. Corbett's strategy was to focus a nation's naval efforts on an

---

[182] Alfred T. Mahan, *The Influence of Sea Power Upon History 1660-1783* (Boston: Little, Brown and Company, 1890), 25-89. This early work (1890) of Mahan significantly influenced the U.S. Navy in its decision to pursue a large battleship fleet, however, by 1906 he was opposed to the mass construction of dreadnought battleship preferring instead a balanced fleet approach; see Alfred T. Mahan, "Reflections, Historic and Other, Suggested by the Battle of the Japan Sea," *Naval Institute Press Proceedings* 32, no. 118 (June 1906): 447-471.

enemy's sea lines of communication and held the belief that by doing so it forced the adversary to seek out that nation's forces to achieve a decisive battle.[183] The shift in thinking resulted in a conclusion that decisive battle was no longer a fleet on fleet battle as had been envisioned by Mahan—and especially his readers—but rather a U-Boat against a convoy escort force. The result being that continued effort over time protecting the lines of communication resulted in a cumulative victory that produced the same results as a decisive battle.[184]

The shift in usage of the submarine initiated by Germany resulted in American naval officers evincing a desire to rapidly develop U.S. offensive submarine capability. As was noted during the beginning of the American war effort, the submarines designed for defensive coastal patrols were less than ideal for the new concept of open ocean submarine operations required by the new German approach. Despite their shortcomings, the U.S. Navy remained focused on smaller submarines based on the introduction of the smaller German UB-class and the UC-class, intended for mining, produced for operations from local bases along the English Channel. This thinking was rapidly embraced by the Board and the U.S. submarine manufacturers but for different reasons. The Board adopted this thinking as a way to rapidly produce a larger number of submarines to conduct coastal operations, thinking that because the Germans had taken this tact and it was proving successful, the United States should also pursue the smaller submarines. The

---

[183] Julian S. Corbett, *Some Principles of Maritime Strategy* (Annapolis, MD: Naval Institute Press, 1911), 183-208; see also William R. Hawkins, "The Man Who Invented Limited War," *Military History Quarterly* 4, no. 1 (Autumn 1991): 432.

[184] Joseph Caldwell Wylie, *Military Strategy: A General Theory of Power Control* (Annapolis, MD: Naval Institute Press, 1967).

Board, while entertaining this concept, was unaware that Germany had already begun to shift away from the smaller U-Boats in favor of the larger Ms U-Boats, the new U-Cruisers, and the large mine laying U-Boats.

The U.S. submarine manufacturers had latched on to the concept of the smaller submarine because for them it meant a higher profit margin since they could continue building the type of submarine they were most familiar with and therefore expend less time and effort on new development designs. The submarine manufacturing establishment went so far as to influence several Navy officers to take their side and to testify before the Board that the smaller type submarine was indeed the course to pursue. This became apparent later as the Navy had to take administrative action against several of these individuals based on their conduct. The submarine force saw the necessity for the larger submarines as had its German counterparts. Key in this story was the influence of Emory S. Land and his consistent drive to pursue the larger submarines, which ultimately won out. The Navy abandoned thoughts of the smaller submarines because Land had demonstrated that the larger submarine was more capable in coastal and open ocean operations.

As the war progressed, the technological development was astounding. The caliber of the personnel brought in to consult and develop technology was second to none. With world class scientists working on the advancement of submarine technology the progress made was noteworthy. The work done by these men laid the foundation of the interwar advances in SONAR, radio, atmospheric control equipment, navigation equipment, and more.

Where the United States ultimately found itself lacking in submarine technology was in the inferiority of its propulsion systems and the unreliability of mechanical equipment. German engineering had produced far superior submarines that were more reliable, longer lasting, and better performing than their American counterparts. It took reverse engineering of the captured and surrendered U-Boats during the early interwar period to allow the United States to finally close this gap.

Finally, the research conducted has raised a few areas that require further research regarding U.S. submarine development, tactics, and doctrine during World War I, to say nothing of similar questions about anti-submarine war developments unique to the U.S. Navy. In particular the development of the SONAR system and the integration of key scientists in the advancement of the technology would require a study all its own. The development of the early atmospheric control equipment discussed in this study could also use some additional research. The mechanism by which U.S. and British ASW development during World War I made the United States so successful against Japanese submarines during World War II would also be worth significant additional research and study. Finally, this study included a more comprehensive examination of the contemporary body of opinion resident in the U.S. Naval Institute *Proceedings* and the discussions therein regarding submarine design and this would also be an area that could use additional study.

As can be seen by this analysis, the impact of the Board on the submarine construction and development during World War I was tremendous. Having a workable design for the submarines as early as 1917, prior to major submarine operations against Germany that came to fruition during the interwar period indicates that the Board was focused on the correct concepts for submarine design despite the U.S. lack of practical experience. The largest shortcomings in U.S. submarines would come from technological inferiority to their German counterparts. With the reverse engineering of German U-Boats, the United States was able to close this gap during the interwar period to make the designs envisioned by the Board a reality. The increased influence of the Navy via the Board on the submarine manufacturing establishment ensured that the U.S. Navy was able to control and direct future development of U.S. submarines ensuring that they met the actual needs of the Navy rather than having to fit the corporate designed submarines for a role they were insufficient to meet. The combined efforts of the Board and key submariners such as Emery S. Land led to a hugely successful interwar advancement of U.S. submarines.

BIBLIOGRAPHY

Archival Sources

Proceedings and Hearings of the General Board of the US Navy, 1900-1950. Archival Information Record Group 80. Combined Arms Research Library, Fort Leavenworth, KS (Microfilm).

Guide to the Scholarly Resources Microfilm Edition of the Hearings before the General Board of the Navy, 1917-50. Wilmington, DE: Scholarly Resources, 1983.

Books

Baer, George W. *One Hundred Years of Sea Power: The US Navy, 1890-1990.* Stanford, CA: Stanford University Press, 1994.

Bond, Brian. *Britain's Two World Wars Against Germany: Myth, Memory and the Distortions of Hindsight.* Cambridge, UK: Cambridge University Press, 2014.

Corbett, Julian S., *Some Principles of Maritime Strategy.* Annapolis, MD: Naval Institute Press, 1911.

Daniels, Josephus. *The Cabinet Diaries of Josephus Daniels, 1913-1921.* Edited by David Cronon. Lincoln: University of Nebraska Press, 1963.

Fiske, Bradley A. *From Midshipman to Rear-Admiral.* New York: The Century Co., 1919.

Friedman, Norman. *Submarine Design and Development.* London, UK: Conway Maritime Press, 1984.

Gleaves, Albert. *Life and Letters of Rear Admiral Stephen B. Luce U. S. Navy Founder of the Naval War College.* New York: The Knickerbocker Press, 1925.

Kuehn, John T. *Agents of Innovation The General Board and the Design of the Fleet That Defeated the Japanese Navy*: Annapolis, MD: Naval Institute Press, 2008.

Mahan, A. T., *The Influence of Sea Power Upon History 1660-1783*, Boston: Little, Brown and Company, 1890.

Rossler, Eberhard. *The U-boat: The Evolution and Technical History of German Submarines.* Translated by Harold Erenbert. Annapolis, MD: Naval Institute Press, 1975.

Weir, Gary E. *Building American Submarines 1914-1940.* Washington, DC: Naval Historical Center Department of the Navy, 1991.

Wylie, Joseph Caldwell. *Military Strategy: A General Theory of Power Control*. Annapolis, MD: Naval Institute Press, 1967.

Periodicals

Alden, Carroll S. "American Submarine Operations in the War." *United States Naval Institute Proceedings* 46, no. 6 (June 1920): 811-850.

Benbow, Tim. "We Cannot Go On: Disruptive Innovation and the First World War Royal Navy." *Security Studies* 19, no. 1 (January 2010): 124-159.

Hawkins, William R. "The Man Who Invented Limited War." *Military History Quarterly* 4, no. 1 (Autumn 1991): 430-436.

Mahan, Alfred T. "Reflections, Historic and Other, Suggested by the Battle of the Japan Sea." *Naval Institute Press Proceedings* 32, no. 118 (June 1906): 447-471.

McGrogan, Don. "USS Bushnell." NavSource Naval History. Accessed 15 February 2017. http://www.navsource.org/archives/09/36/3602.htm.

Naval History and Heritage Command. "Dictionary of American Naval Fighting Ships—Index." US Navy. Accessed 10 April 2017. https://www.history.navy.mil/research/histories/ship-histories/danfs.html.

Williams, William. "Josephus Daniels and the US Navy's Shipbuilding Program in World War I." *The Journal of Military History* 60, no. 1 (January 1996) 7-38.

www.ingramcontent.com/pod-product-compliance
Lightning Source LLC
Chambersburg PA
CBHW080924170426
43201CB00016B/2258